RECENT RESEARCHES IN THE MUSIC OF THE BAROQUE ERA • VOLUME IV

Jean-Marie Leclair

SONATAS FOR VIOLIN AND BASSO CONTINUO

Opus 5, Opus 9, and Opus 15
Part I: Opus 5, Sonatas I–V

Edited by Robert E. Preston

A-R EDITIONS, INC. • NEW HAVEN

© 1968, A-R Editions, Inc.

For Sylvia

Contents

Preface

    The Composer and His Works   ix

    The Sonatas for Violin and Basso Continuo   x

    Stylistic Qualities of the Sonatas   xi

    Leclair's Notation   xiii

    Ornamentation   xv

    Bowing   xxii

    Editorial Practice   xxiv

    Notes   xxvi

Opus 5, Sonatas I-V

    Sonata I   1

    Sonata II   14

    Sonata III   26

    Sonata IV   43

    Sonata V   65

Preface

The Composer and His Works

Lionel de La Laurencie gives a detailed and carefully documented account of Leclair's life in the first volume of his monumental work, *L'École française de violon*.[1] A more recent book, Marc Pincherle's *Jean-Marie Leclair l'aîné*, contains a biographical chapter which brings the La Laurencie work up to date.[2] These two sources incorporate all of the reliable information about Leclair's life that is presently available.

Jean-Marie Leclair was born in Lyon on May 10, 1697, the eldest of eight children.[3] He learned the trade of lacemaking, and at the time of his first marriage, in 1716, he qualified as a *maître passementier*. Leclair was also a dancer; prior to their marriage both he and his wife danced at the Lyon opera. In 1722 he was engaged as first dancer and ballet master at the Turin opera, where he composed a few short pieces for the ballet. His stay in Turin was short; in 1723 he went to Paris, where he soon published his *Premier livre de sonates à violon seul avec la basse continue*, Opus 1. Leclair remained in Paris probably for two or three years, and then returned to Turin.

Quantz notes Leclair's presence in Turin in 1726 and mentions that Leclair was taking violin lessons from the director of the royal orchestra, Giovanni Battista Somis.[4] In 1728 Leclair returned to Paris and made his debut at the *Concerts spirituels*,[5] the first of the many performances he presented there until about 1736. Around the year of his return to Paris, 1728, he published his *Second livre de sonates pour le violon et pour le flûte traversière avec la basse continue*, Opus 2, engraved by Louise Catherine Roussel. The title misleadingly implies that the works are trio sonatas; they are, rather, solo sonatas, several of which were written for alternative performance on the flute. Opus 3, *Sonates à deux violons sans basse*, appeared in 1730, as did Opus 4, *Sonates en trio pour deux violons et la basse continue*. The date of the death of Leclair's first wife is unknown, but in 1730 the composer married Louise Roussel, who engraved all his remaining works, including two posthumous sonatas. Among the witnesses at their wedding was André Cheron, with whom Leclair had studied composition.[6]

By 1734 Leclair had achieved considerable fame through his performances at the *Concerts spirituels* and was summoned into the service of Louis XV as *premier symphoniste du Roi*. Opus 5, *Troisième livre de sonates à violon seul avec la basse continue*, composed about 1734, is dutifully dedicated to Louis. Marpurg tells an amusing tale of Leclair's leaving the king's service rather than play second violin in the orchestra.[7] Whether or not the account is accurate, Leclair had in any case left his royal post by 1736, and had also ceased playing at the *Concerts spirituels*, although his compositions were still performed there by others. About 1737 Leclair published three more works: Opus 6, *Première récréation de musique, d'une exécution facile, composée pour deux violons et la basse continue;* Opus 7, *Six concerto à tre violini, alto, e basso per organo e violoncello;* and Opus 8, *Deuxième récréation de musique d'une exécution facile, composée pour deux flûtes ou deux violons et la basse continue*. In or about the following year he published Opus 9, *Quatrième livre de sonates à violon seul avec la basse continue*.

Leclair made at least one extended journey to Holland, but the precise dates of his trip have never been ascertained. He may have arrived there as early as 1737. François du Liz, a wealthy art patron,[8] hired Leclair as his music director in 1740, and Leclair lived at du Liz's residence in The Hague for two years.

Leclair also stayed in Leeuwarden at the court of Princess Anne of Orange, from whom he received the *Croix du Lion Néerlandais*; it has not been determined whether his engagement with the princess preceded or followed the one with François du Liz. Leclair had certainly known the princess before 1738, because his Opus 9, published in or about that year, is dedicated to her. Several of Leclair's early biographers assert that he made the trip to Holland intending to study with Locatelli; no proof exists, however, that Leclair ever met Locatelli, much less that he became his student.[9]

By 1743 Leclair had returned to Paris, but only a short time passed before he was summoned to the court of Don Philippe, *infante* of Spain. In 1743 or 1744 Leclair dedicated his Opus 10, *VI concerti à tre violini, alto, e basso per organo e violoncello*, to this prince. In 1744 Leclair was again in Paris, where he remained for the rest of his life.

Leclair's only opera, *Scylla et Glaucus*, Opus 11, was performed in 1746 with considerable success. In the following year Leclair published his Opus 12, *Second livre de sonates à deux violons sans basse*. In 1748 or 1749 the Duke of Gramont, a former pupil of Leclair's who had known him for many years, hired him as first violinist of the ducal orchestra. In this post Leclair composed a few pieces, all of them now lost, intended for use as incidental music to various operas. In about 1753 Leclair's *Ouvertures et sonates en trio pour deux violons avec la basse continue*, Opus 13, was published. This curious work consists largely of trio-sonata arrangements of Leclair's own earlier compositions.

In 1758 Leclair and his wife separated and moved to new addresses. Leclair bought a house in a suburb of Paris, where he lived alone until his death. Pincherle describes the location as "secluded, sinister to the point of arousing the liveliest apprehensions among Leclair's friends."[10] The Duke of Gramont, among others, offered Leclair permanent lodging, but he preferred to remain alone. On the night of October

23, 1764, Leclair was stabbed to death; his assassin was never found. La Laurencie cites in detail the police records, including the inquest, and other information pertaining to Leclair's death, as well as some rather violent statements made about Leclair by his nephew, a violinist of small talent whom Leclair had on various occasions refused to help.[11] In referring to Leclair's death, several contemporary writers used the term *assassiné*, suggesting that intrigue played a part in his murder. Several eighteenth-century sources state that Leclair was killed on his way home, a curious misstatement in light of the official police records, which clearly indicate that the murder was done in Leclair's house.

Leclair was buried in Paris on October 25, 1764, at the church of Saint-Laurent. On December 2 a memorial service was held at the church of the Feuillants on the Rue Saint-Honoré; the orchestra and chorus, including members of the *Concerts spirituels*, performed Mondonville's motet *De Profundis* and Leclair's "Le Tombeau" (the sixth sonata from Opus 5), which had been arranged as a *grande symphonie* by Dupont of the Royal Academy of Music, one of Leclair's pupils.

Leclair's widow engraved two posthumous works, *Trio pour deux violons et basse*, in 1766, and *Sonate à violon seul et basse continue*, in 1767. Both works bear the designation *ouvrage postume*, but are generally listed as Opus 14 and Opus 15.

The Sonatas for Violin and Basso Continuo

Michel Corrette, in the preface to one of his treatises on accompaniment, discusses the introduction of Italian music into France at the end of the seventeenth century and states that French musicians were at first unable to perform Italian sonatas. Corrette speaks of a concert given by M. Mathieu, curate of the church of St. André des Arts:

It was at this concert that the trios [trio sonatas] of Corelli, printed in Rome, appeared for the first time. This new kind of music encouraged all composers to work in a more brilliant style; such was the *Caprice* of Mr. Rebel the elder.[12] All concerts took on a different form; scenes and symphonies from operas were replaced by sonatas; . . . .[13]

. . . During the same period Corelli wrote his Opus 5 [the solo sonatas written in 1700], a masterpiece of the art [of composition]. The late Duke of Orleans (who later became the Regent of the Realm), being very much interested in music, wished to hear these sonatas, but since he was unable to find a single violinist in all of Paris capable of playing in double stops, he was obliged to have them sung by three voices. But this lack of violinists did not last long. Each [violinist] worked day and night at learning these sonatas, with the result that in a few years three violinists who could perform them emerged: Chatillon, who was also an organist, [François] Duval, and Baptiste [Jean-Baptiste Anet]. The latter made a journey to Rome for the sole purpose of hearing these sonatas played by the composer himself.

One can judge from the number of fine violinists now in Paris how much progress music has made since the invention of the sonata, for symphonies from operas would never have produced such great artists.[14]

Corrette's rather startling claim that the Duke of Orleans was obliged "to have them [the Corelli solo sonatas] sung by three voices"[15] may be false, but his assertion that these sonatas provided an important impetus to the writing of solo sonatas in France is entirely correct. Pincherle states that between 1692 and 1715 about twenty-five collections of sonatas were published in Paris.[16] Most of these were written by Italians residing in France or by Frenchmen who had studied in Italy. Early in the century, French composers, including Jean-Fery Rebel, François Duval, and Jean-Baptiste Senallié, wrote sonatas for violin and basso continuo.[17] The French sonatas improve in quality and increase greatly in quantity during the second decade of the eighteenth century, as exemplified in the works of Louis Francoeur and Jacques Aubert.

The basic form of the sonata, including the number and types of its movements, was well established during the first twenty years of the eighteenth century. Composers wrote fewer and fewer sonatas with programmatic titles or connotations, and made increasing use of titles which suggest tempos, sometimes including additional expressive indications. The sharp distinction between the *sonata da camera* and *sonata da chiesa* gradually became blurred, to the extent that by Leclair's time it was negligible. Leclair himself made tremendous strides in developing the internal character of the individual movements of the sonata and in the expansion of violin technique,[18] but he stands more as the perfecter of a style then as an innovator, since the violin sonata as an important French form was firmly established well before the publication of Leclair's first book of sonatas in 1723.

It is surprising that this, the first book (Opus 1), was published in Paris, although the composer was definitely in Lyon and Turin until 1722. Apparently within the short space of a year Leclair went to Paris, found a worthy patron, secured a *privilège général*, and had the work published. Opus 1 contains twelve sonatas, as do the three later books of sonatas for violin and continuo. The second book appeared about 1728; although an opus number does not appear on its title page, Leclair referred to it as Opus 2 in the catalogues of his works which appeared at a later date.

The two remaining books of sonatas comprise the present edition, and require detailed description. The third book, Opus 5, appeared about 1734. The title page reads:

Third book of sonatas for solo violin and basso continuo. Composed by Mr. Leclair the elder, ordinary of the music of the Chapel and of the King's chamber. Engraved by Madame Leclair, his wife. Dedicated to the King [Louis XV]. Opus V. Price 12 pounds. [Sold] in Paris: at the home of the composer, St. Benoist Street near the door of the Abbey of St. Germain; [at the shop of] the widow Boivin, St. Honoré Street at the Golden Rule; [and at the shop of] Mr. Leclerc, Roule Street at the Golden Cross. With the privilege of the King.[19]

This volume was written shortly after Leclair had entered

the service of Louis XV and bears a flowery dedication typical of its time:

Sire:

The favor which Your Majesty has just conferred upon me permits the homage that I venture to render to you. For the first time I bring to your feet the fruits of a domestic muse. How glorious this title is for me! The ardent desire to be worthy of it one day has sustained my weakness in the face of an art which is long and painful [to learn]; the good fortune of success has fulfilled my ambition. The work of my whole life is more than paid for by the moments in which Your Majesty has condescended to lend an ear to my music. These moments, always precious, are even more so at the present time,[20] but perhaps Your Majesty will recall that the times of conquest of the late King [Louis XIV] were those of the greatest progress in our art. The glory of the sovereign influences the genius of his subjects. It is natural that a nation under your rule should yield supremacy to no other people in pleasurable accomplishments, any more than in useful or necessary ones. I am, with the most profound respect, Sire, the very humble, very obedient, and very faithful subject and servant of Your Majesty.

J.-M. Leclair, the elder.[21]

The fourth book, Opus 9, appeared about 1738. The title page reads:

Fourth book of sonatas for solo violin with basso continuo. Composed by Mr. Leclair the Elder. Engraved by Madame Leclair, his wife. Dedicated to Her Royal Highness, Madame the Princess of Orange. Opus IX. Price 15 pounds. [Sold] in Paris: at the home of the composer, St. Benoist Street near the door of the Abbey of St. Germain; [at the shop of] the widow Boivin, St. Honoré Street at the Golden Rule; [and at the shop of] Mr. Leclerc, Roule Street at the Golden Cross. With the privilege of the King.[22]

The dedication reads:

To Her Royal Highness, Madame the Princess of Orange
Madame:

The taste of Your Royal Highness for the true beauties of music, and the profound knowledge which you have of the principles of the art, are not the only motives which have inspired in me the confidence to offer you this work. I know that, not content with loving all talents, you take pride in protecting them. I experienced this, Madame, during all the time that I spent at your Court, where you had done me the honor of calling me. Applause is the most flattering reward of the arts; the memory of that which I have received from Your Royal Highness is more precious to me than the memory of your acts of kindness. All my life I will make renewed efforts to justify it. I am, Madame, with the most respectful devotion, the very humble and very obedient servant of Your Royal Highness.

Le Clair the elder.[23]

The *Avertissement* in the fourth book is of considerable importance.

All those who wish to succeed in performing this work in the spirit of the author must devote themselves to discovering the character of each piece as well as the correct tempo and the quality of sound appropriate to the different pieces. An important point, on which one cannot lay too much stress, is to avoid the confusion of notes that are sometimes added to melodic and expressive passages, and which serve only to disfigure them. It is no less ridiculous to change the tempo of two rondos which are written [to follow] one another, and to play the major one faster than the minor one. It is fine to enliven the major by one's manner of playing it, but this can be done without accelerating the beat.

I am too much obliged to connoisseurs and to the public for the flattering praise with which they have honored me for so long, to have spared either the time or the care needed to render this work both instructive and pleasing. I dare to hope that people will not think ill of me that I am selling this book for 15 pounds, and that in the future the preceding books will be sold only at the same price, 15 pounds, because of the considerable expense I have undertaken in restoring a number of plates which were entirely worn out.[24]

Detailed reference to this important *Avertissement* will be made in my discussion of ornamentation, beginning on page xvi, below.

The posthumous solo sonata, Opus 15, was published in 1767.[25] The title page reads:

Sonata for solo violin and basso continuo. Posthumous opus of Mr. Leclair the elder. Engraved by his widow. Price 1 pound, 16 sols. [Sold] in Paris: at the home of the widow Leclair, in the wide part of the Street of the Four St. Germain, in the home of Mr. Chavagnac, master mason and contractor; and at the usual addresses of [vendors of] music. [Sold] in Lyon [at the shop of] Mr. Castaud, Square of the Comedie. With the privilege of the King. Printed by Maillet.[26]

The title page is followed by a catalogue of Leclair's works which includes the two posthumous sonatas.[27]

Leclair's first two books of sonatas are available in modern editions.[28] The third and fourth books and the posthumous solo sonata have never been republished in modern times—the *raison d'être* of the present edition. Single sonatas from all four books have appeared from time to time, but few of them are still in print. Several of the sonatas that remain in print, especially those issued during the first decade of the twentieth century, represent virtual adaptations or arrangements of Leclair's music, rather than editions faithful to their sources.

Stylistic Qualities of the Sonatas

Of the twelve sonatas in Leclair's first book, nine have four movements, two have three, and one has five. All the four-movement sonatas are cast in the tempo scheme slow-fast-slow-fast. Dances such as the allemande, the musette, the sarabande, the gavotte, the minuet, and the gigue mingle with non-dance movements. Of Leclair's numerous designs for individual movements the most common is a two-part form in which each part is repeated, and in which the second part always contains at least a brief thematic reference to the first. In some movements the second half brings back nearly all of the principal thematic material of the first; in others it consists almost entirely of new material. Monopartite, tripartite, fugal, and rondo structures also appear in the first book. The harmonic vocabulary is rather conservative, almost entirely diatonic apart from secondary dominants and a few diminished-seventh chords. In its demands on violin technique the first book is much more conservative than the third and fourth.

In the second book, again, nine sonatas have four movements, two have three, and one has five. A ground bass provides the structure of the opening *Adagio* of the first sonata; otherwise there are no new formal structures in this book. It is in the realm of harmony that the second book makes its most significant advances over the first.[29] Augmented-sixth, diminished-seventh, and Neapolitan chords are used frequently. The latter sonority nearly always includes a major seventh that makes the chord more poignant. The book presents many unusual, and some startling, harmonic progressions. Perhaps the most significant are the many avoided or deceptive cadences, in which a dominant chord resolves to one of a wide assortment of non-diatonic chords. Disruptive harmonic progressions are often accompanied by unusual melodic leaps which intensify their impact. By and large, the violin writing in the second book is no more difficult than that in the first book.

In general the treatment of harmony in the third book is not so bold or imaginative as in the second. Delayed or avoided cadences, used very effectively in the second book, are seldom found in the third. Although chromatic chords such as the augmented-sixth and Neapolitan are scarce, the range of modulation within a given movement is wider than in the earlier books. Leclair makes increasing use of a harmonic technique that might be termed "bimodality," in which a piece written in the major mode borrows a single chord, or occasionally several chords, from the opposite—the minor—mode, or vice versa. Occasionally a passage of several measures may borrow all its harmony from the opposite mode, producing an unusual coloristic effect.

The third book makes more technical demands on the violinist than its predecessors do, particularly in several slow movements which utilize double stops from beginning to end. Sonata 12 far exceeds the limit of technical difficulty of any previous sonata.

The sonatas of the fourth book also contain four movements. The tempo scheme slow-fast-slow-fast is found in all the sonatas except the sixth, in which the normal order of the first two movements is reversed. Two new dances are introduced in the fourth book, the courante and the corrente.

A wider variety of melody types occurs in the fourth book than in the third. A number of movements present a general melodic contour—for example, widely spaced chord-outlines—rather than specific themes. Several movements, both fast and slow, utilize one or more motives as a basic melodic source; although it is not new in the fourth book, this procedure is much more common there than in any of the earlier books.

A basic change of texture distinguishes the fourth book from the earlier books: the continuo line often loses most of its melodic significance and becomes merely a harmonic bass, a turn away from baroque style towards the rococo.

Several notable differences appear in the harmonic style of the fourth book. Dominant chords in the continuo are occasionally supplemented in the violin part by ninths, elevenths, or thirteenths, often approached and left by skip. In earlier books such dissonances occur seldom and are used only as passing tones. In the first three books Leclair almost never modulates to keys with more than four sharps or flats, but in the fourth he occasionally moves to keys with as many as six. A few movements, in particular the third movements of Sonatas 5 and 9, are extremely chromatic, with modulations in almost every measure. Chromaticism is perhaps to be expected in the developmental portions of a movement, but in the fourth book a number of the principal themes themselves are markedly chromatic. A few opening themes are tonally ambiguous; others contain a cadence in a key other than the expected tonic. As a rule, the opening themes of movements in the fourth book do not conclude with an authentic cadence.

Leclair's treatment of mode in the fourth book is significantly different from that found in the earlier books. Although passages which borrow their harmony from the opposite mode have been noted in the third book, they are presented there as events significant in themselves, usually heralded by a change of key signature. Not until the fourth book does bimodality seem implicit in Leclair's harmonic thinking. Individual chords, especially the tonic, supertonic, subdominant and submediant chords, are freely borrowed from the opposite mode. The minor dominant may substitute for the expected major. For instance, the opening *Adagio* of Sonata 1 is written in A major. The first half concludes in E major, but only after a lengthy section in E minor. The second half returns to the tonic A major, but only after a considerable span in A minor. Thus, the tonic and dominant tonalities appear in both major and minor forms. It is impossible to predict which mode will appear at each stage of a modulatory sequence. The extraordinary range of modulations and many of the modulations themselves are accomplished through bimodal means. In one instance the minor mode is implied by the violin line at a point where the major mode is suggested by the continuo (see measures 10–11 in the *Allegro ma non troppo* of Sonata 7). In several sonatas, the mode momentarily alternates between major and minor over the same bass note.

In creating the fourth book Leclair sought to widen the expressive and idiomatic possibilities of his instrument; thus the book makes considerably greater demands on violin technique than its predecessors do. The most important advance is in the more frequent use of difficult double stops, often involving real contrapuntal movement between voices. Leaps in double stops are found much more often than in earlier books. Scale passages in which many staccatos are grouped under one bow occur in many of the sonatas in the fourth book, rarely in the earlier sonatas.

The fourth book makes greater use than the others of the extreme upper register of the violin, particularly in Sonata 8, where one passage rises as high as c''''. Quick violinistic figurations involving leaps of a tenth are common, as are figurations requiring difficult string crossings and awkward hand positions. Both scale and broken-chord flourishes of considerable technical difficulty are present in most of these sonatas. Emphasis on virtuoso display reaches a height in the opening *Allegro* of Sonata 6, in which the violinist is asked to play on three strings simultaneously with an additional, rapid *tremblement* on the middle string.

In all four books of sonatas, the increasing complexity of Leclair's idiomatic writing is sharply set off by the persistent appearance of sonatas written to be played on either the violin or the flute. Five of the twelve sonatas in the second book are written for flute or violin, and even the fourth book contains two sonatas of this type. In writing sonatas for either violin or flute Leclair probably had the financial object of inducing flutists to buy his works. He was, however, first of all a violinist, and the sonatas written for alternate performance on the flute are generally not so successful as those written for the violin alone—not simply because of the narrower range and lack of double stops in the flute sonatas, but rather because Leclair's imagination seems less fettered in the violin sonatas. The highly expressive *Adagio* movements from Sonatas 5 and 9 in the fourth book contain few double stops and seldom exceed the lower range of the flute, yet both sonatas are written exclusively for the violin.

Leclair's works bring virtuoso writing and harmonic ingenuity to a climax in the history of the eighteenth-century French violin sonata. The sonatas of his immediate French successors—Guignon, Mondonville, Dauvergne, l'Abbe le fils, and Travernol—are harmonically much more conservative, and rarely approach, much less exceed, the limits of virtuosity demanded by Leclair. This is surprising; several of these composers were famed virtuosos, doubtless capable of performing music of extraordinary difficulty. The sonatas of Gabriel Guillemain are exceptional; in his first book (1734) Guillemain surpasses Leclair in the use of difficult violin techniques without, however, resorting to the somewhat bizarre acrobatics one often encounters in the solo sonatas of Locatelli.

The diversity of style in Leclair's sonatas is accompanied, it must be admitted, by a certain unevenness of quality. Some of the fast movements in particular seem more contrived than inspired, more routine than exciting. But among the sonatas are many movements of extraordinary beauty and expressiveness, which earn for Leclair a prominent place among the finest eighteenth-century composers for the violin.

Leclair's Notation

Leclair's notation deviates in several important ways from the usual practices of the mid-eighteenth century, especially in the use of accidentals and in the figuring of the bass. In general, Leclair's accidentals apply for only one beat, or to notes grouped together rhythmically. Even when a raised (or lowered) note obviously remains altered, the sharp (or flat) sign is usually repeated, as in the following example.

Opus 5, Sonata 1, *Allegro*, measure 9

Example 1

Accidentals are not repeated consistently, however. In the following passage, for instance, c″ sharp is carefully reindicated throughout measure 17, but is not indicated on the last beat of measure 18.

Opus 5, Sonata 11, *Allegro*, measures 17–18

Example 2

In a movement with a signature of one or more flats, a note affected by the key signature may be raised by either a natural sign or a sharp sign. The sharp sign is favored over the natural sign, particularly when the raised note is a leading tone. These two signs are not used with any consistency; even within the same movement a pitch may be designated one way in the violin and a different way in the bass. Occasionally, a note inflected by the key signature is raised (by either a sharp or a natural sign) and subsequently lowered within the same measure. The lowering of the second note is often indicated merely by the absence of any accidental sign; the performer is expected to assume that the note returns to its natural (that is, its lowered) state.

In a movement with a signature of one or more sharps, a note inflected by the key signature is lowered by a flat rather than a natural—a usage that is especially confusing to the modern performer when the note is first lowered and then raised in the same measure. The lowered note is preceded by a flat and the raised one by a natural. By the natural sign Leclair intends to convey that the note is to be played in its "natural" state, which, because of the key signature, happens to be sharp. Thus, a melodic line written:

Opus 1, Sonata 12, *Allegro ma non troppo*, measure 25

Example 3

would be played:

Example 4

Accidentals which apply to notes not inflected by the key signature are usually treated still differently. Regardless whether the signature consists of sharps or flats, the natural, sharp, and flat signs before notes unaffected by the signature convey their conventional modern meanings.

By way of summary, a few general principles may be stated about Leclair's handling of accidentals. A sharp sign always means that its note is to be raised, and a flat sign always means that its note is to be lowered. The natural sign may cancel an accidental, as in modern usage, or it may mean that a note which was previously lowered is to return to its "natural" inflection within the key designated by the key signature of the movement. The mere absence of an accidental sign before a note previously sharped or flatted within the same measure indicates the cancellation of the preceding accidental. To temper these general rules, however, it must be emphasized that Leclair's treatment of accidentals, like his presentation of pitches and rhythmic values, incorporates many errors that are probably the result of simple carelessness.

Leclair's use of accidentals clearly poses problems to an initial reading of his sonatas from the original editions. Fortunately, careful study of the music leaves few serious doubts; the solution to a question of inflection is usually apparent when one has sufficient time to consider the problematic passage in its musical context.

Leclair's figured basses also present problems of interpretation. The composer's method of figuring was, it seems, a kind of personal shorthand, reflecting no apparent concern that his practice showed but faint resemblance to that of his contemporaries.[30] First of all, Leclair's treatment of the accidentals accompanying the figures is confusing. The symbols ♯ and ✕ (or ♯3 and ✕3) are used interchangeably throughout all four books; the usage is misleading, since a number of other composers use ✕ only to indicate a double sharp.

A third or a sixth not inflected by the key signature is raised or lowered by conventional means— ♯3, ♯6, ♭3, or ♭6, for example. The figures ♯3 and ♯6 are also used, however, to indicate that a third or a sixth is to be raised by canceling an accidental in the key signature. Conversely, if a third or a sixth is to be lowered by canceling an accidental in the key signature, the inflection is usually indicated by the figure ♭3 or ♭6. The sign ♮ usually means that a note should be sounded in its "natural" state—that is, its diatonic inflection. Thus, in a piece in G major the note D accompanied by ♮ (or ♮3) indicates an F sharp over the bass; if F natural were desired, it would be designated by ♭ (or ♭3).

In the violin line Leclair occasionally uses the sign ※ to indicate a double sharp. In the figured bass, however, he uses no such special sign but rather a simple sharp sign, ♯ or ✕. Double-sharped notes occur only in movements with several sharps in the key signature. In such movements, the bass note D sharp accompanied by the symbol ♯ (or ✕), for example, indicates an F✕ over the bass.

The figure 2 by itself usually accompanies a note which resolves downward to a ⁶₅ chord. A chord with the figure 2 should be realized with a fourth and a sixth, in addition to the second, over the bass note. When Leclair wants a fifth as well as a second over the bass, he uses the figure ⁵₂.

The figure ♯2 nearly always indicates the third inversion of a diminished-seventh chord. Occasionally the completion of the diminished-seventh chord requires the alteration of another interval over the bass—the augmentation of the fourth over the bass, for example. Nevertheless, Leclair seldom includes the figures which are theoretically necessary to specify all the necessary chromatic alterations in the diminished-seventh chord, since the figure ♯2 is nearly always intended to indicate an entire chord structure rather than a simple interval.

The figure ♯4 indicates the third inversion of a dominant-seventh chord. Here again a figure is used to denote an entire chord structure, and Leclair assumes that the keyboard performer will supply any and all chromatic alterations which may be necessary to complete the chord.

Leclair assumes that in root-position chords all fifths above the bass are to be perfect, even though this may necessitate the supplying of a chromatic alteration (a raising or lowering) of the fifth. Occasionally, when the fifth above the bass must be lowered to become perfect, Leclair uses the figure ♭5; the figure 5̸, never ♭5, is used to indicate a diminished fifth. Similarly, the figure ♭4, which occurs only in connection with other figures (e.g., ♭⁶₄₃), indicates a perfect, not a diminished, fourth.

The figure 5̸ by itself always indicates a first-inversion dominant-seventh chord. Since the figure represents a specific chord rather than a single interval above the bass, Leclair seldom bothers to indicate other alterations which may be necessary to create the chord, such as the raised third over the bass in Example 5.

Occasionally, if the sixth over the bass must be raised to create the diminished-seventh chord, Leclair uses the figure ♯6/5̸. In denoting a dominant-seventh chord, however, he never includes the figure 6 with the figure 5̸.

Diminished triads occur infrequently and are indicated by ⁸⁄5̸.

In the *Avertissement* to his first book of sonatas Leclair explains that he will use the figure 6 to indicate a ⁶₄₃ chord,

xiv

Example 5

and that a raised or lowered sixth in this chord will be shown by ♯6 or ♭6. In the *Avertissement* to his second book Leclair states that he will no longer use the slash through the figure 6 to indicate the $\begin{smallmatrix}6\\4\\3\end{smallmatrix}$ chord. Throughout the second, third, and fourth books, chords of this type are usually indicated simply by the figure 6; the complete spelling is given only when one or more notes in the chord are altered, as in, for example, $\begin{smallmatrix}6\\4\\\sharp 3\end{smallmatrix}$ or $\begin{smallmatrix}6\\\flat 4\\\flat 3\end{smallmatrix}$. The figure 6 can, then, have two possible meanings, $\begin{smallmatrix}6\\3\end{smallmatrix}$ or $\begin{smallmatrix}6\\4\\3\end{smallmatrix}$, and only from the context can one determine which is the more appropriate.[31] In many instances both chords seem correct and the decision to use one or the other is arbitrary.

The figure 7 by itself implies an unaltered seventh over the bass, regardless whether the seventh is major or minor. It also presupposes a perfect fifth above the bass. If the fifth is to be diminished, Leclair usually uses the figure $\begin{smallmatrix}7\\\flat 5\end{smallmatrix}$.

Leclair's figuring of the diminished-seventh chord is inconsistent. The chord poses no problem when it occurs in any inversion, since the intervals are usually specified, as shown in the following example.

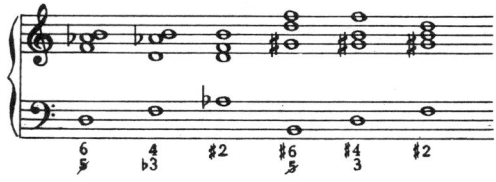

Example 6

In the root position, however, the chord is figured in several different ways. The most usual indication is 7; this figure refers to an entire chord structure rather than to the simple interval of the diminished seventh over the bass, and therefore Leclair almost never specifies other, implicit alterations.

The figure ♭7 is frequently used in situations in which the seventh needs to be lowered by an accidental for the creation of a diminished interval. The flat sign is frequently omitted, however, and the figure 7 is assumed to indicate a diminished seventh. Occasionally the slash through the 7 is omitted, and the chord is indicated by ♭7 Only from its context can one determine whether ♭7 designates the diminished-seventh chord or the interval of a minor seventh to be added over a diatonic triad.

Ornamentation

The problem of ornamentation in eighteenth-century music is exceedingly complex, even when one is dealing with a piece of French keyboard music prefaced by a convenient table of *agréments*. In the Leclair violin sonatas, however, as in most violin music of their time, only a few basic symbols for ornaments are used, and it becomes especially difficult to prescribe a precise execution for each ornament.

In his doctoral dissertation, Putnam Aldrich gives probably the most careful, clear, and complete study that has ever been made of the problem of ornamentation in seventeenth- and eighteenth-century music.[32] The present commentary contains many references to Aldrich's work as it pertains to the Leclair sonatas, but does not purport to be a summary of his findings.

The first problem confronting the performer of much baroque music is to determine where ornaments should be placed; in Leclair's sonatas their placement is, as I shall argue below, clearly specified. Leclair uses only two basic ornamental signs, the small note, ♪, written as an eighth note,[33] and the small cross, +. Both signs occur frequently, and each is used, apparently, to designate several different kinds of ornaments.

Some scholars advance the argument that ornaments often were not specifically called for in baroque music because competent performers were expected to know where and how to add them. This reasoning may apply to some composers but not, I believe, to Leclair. My position is supported, first of all, by Quantz, who clearly states that although the ornamentation of Italian music was often left entirely to the discretion of the performer, it was part of French baroque practice to specify the location of all ornaments.[34]

The view that Leclair meticulously specifies ornamentation is consistent with the fact that his sonatas are on the whole carefully edited—as illustrated, for example, by his use of accidentals. I have explained previously that Leclair's accidentals apply for only one beat; when the reiteration of a chromatic inflection is required, the accidental is faithfully repeated, even in situations leaving no possible doubt that the note should remain altered, as in the following fragment:

Example 7

In this instance the composer could certainly have relied on the performer to repeat the alteration. It often seems, though, that the more obvious the alteration, the more likely Leclair is to specify it carefully. My opinion is that Leclair trusted the discretion of the performer no more in the placement of ornaments than in the use of accidentals.

In eighteenth-century France, the final decision regarding all problems of ornamentation was considered to rest with *le bon goût*, the good taste, of the performer.[35] Aldrich writes, "It was *goût* which should regulate not only the quantity of *agréments* to be used, but the interpretation of each individual ornament—the duration of each appoggiatura, the number of oscillations in each trill."[36] He continues, "Even before the middle of the eighteenth century there must have been a tendency, on the part of some French performers, to exceed the limits of *bon goût*, to sacrifice refinement and expressiveness for the sake of speed and brilliance."[37]

To redress this unfortunate condition, Leclair gives some stern advice to the performer in the first paragraph of the *Avertissement* to his fourth book of sonatas:

All those who wish to succeed in performing this work in the spirit of the author must devote themselves to discovering the character of each piece as well as the correct tempo and the quality of sound appropriate to the different pieces. An important point, on which one cannot lay too much stress, is to avoid the confusion of notes that are sometimes added to melodic and expressive passages, and which serve only to disfigure them. It is no less ridiculous to change the tempo of two rondos which are written [to follow] one another, and to play the major one faster than the minor one. It is fine to enliven the major by one's manner of playing it, but this can be done without accelerating the beat.[38]

The opening of this *Avertissement* is a simple appeal to the performer to use his *bon goût*—to determine the real character and tempo of each piece before attempting to perform it. A precise translation of the next part of the original French, especially the phrase *morceaux de chant et d'expression* (which I have provisionally rendered as "melodic and expressive passages"),[39] is difficult if not impossible, but the general meaning of the passage seems clear: Leclair is admonishing the performer to avoid adding free embellishment. The advice is extremely important since it runs counter to the well-established baroque practice of making simple slow movements highly ornate and rhapsodic in actual performance. Leclair's statement lends weight to the argument that ornaments are rarely necessary other than where they are specified; his obvious concern about the danger of too much ornamentation would logically have led him to indicate precisely where he did want ornaments performed.

Although it is not directly related to the problem of ornamentation, the remainder of Leclair's *Avertissement* deserves special comment. The warning against changes of tempo refers to certain movements in a tripartite form, in which each part constitutes a small rondo: A B A C A / D E D F D / A. The first part of such movements usually centers around one mode and the middle section around the opposite mode. Leclair insists that the tempo remain constant throughout the movement. In addition to the three-part movements, the sonatas include a few movements in the major mode that contain extended sections in the minor mode—the chaconnes, for example; Leclair's instructions apply to these as well.

Apparently a number of people misunderstood this *Avertissement*, because Leclair felt it necessary to add further advice at a later date. In the *Avertissement* to his Opus 13, *Overtures et Sonates en trio . . .*, Leclair writes:

I beg that performers will not find fault if I remind them of the *Avertissement* at the head of my fourth book of sonatas. I neglected to say that by the term *Allegro* I by no means intend a movement which is very fast; I intend a gay movement. Those who quicken it too much, especially in forceful pieces such as most of the fugues in $\frac{4}{4}$ time, render the melody trivial, instead of preserving its nobility. This advice is directed only to persons who may have need of it.[40]

A few performers must have played Leclair's allegros excessively fast, or the composer would not have thought it necessary to add this somewhat sarcastic note of warning.

In light of the preceding discussion it seems safe to conclude that in the Leclair sonatas ornaments are necessary only where they are called for. Two problems remain: how is each ornament indicated, and how should it be performed? In the following paragraphs each of Leclair's ornaments will be discussed briefly and one or two possible realizations will be suggested. Numerous possible realizations exist for nearly every ornament; if a complete discussion of any ornament is desired, the reader is referred to the Aldrich dissertation. To simplify references to that work, I shall take up the following topics in the order that Aldrich assigns them.

The *single appoggiatura approached from below* (or, as in Aldrich, "the single inferior appoggiatura"), usually called the *port de voix*, consists of a note which lies a major or minor second below the principal note. Leclair indicates it with a small note:

Example 8

Eighteenth-century sources differ as to whether this note should be played during the time of the preceding note or that of the main (the following) note. The best solution for the Leclair sonatas, in my opinion, is to perform the note during the time of the main note, and to hold it for about half the value of that note.[41] French sources do not mention how long the *port de voix* should be held when it is followed by a dotted note, but its duration should certainly be governed by the tempo and character of the movement. In most instances it is appropriate, I think, to hold such a *port de voix* for the value of the main note, letting the main note itself receive the value of the dot. Several sources mention a *port de voix feint*, in which the lower note is held for almost the whole time of the main note. The sources agree that any *port de voix* must be played in the same bow stroke as the main note.

The *single appoggiatura approached from above* ("the single superior appoggiatura") appears as (a) a suspension of a second above the main note, (b) a middle note between two notes of the melody that form the interval of a descending third, and (c) an unprepared appoggiatura one degree above the main note and approached from any interval. Leclair indicates the single superior appoggiatura, in all three forms, with a small note:

Example 9

The appoggiatura is always performed in the same bow stroke as the main note. Aldrich presents a series of examples showing that from the end of the seventeenth century into the first decade of the eighteenth century the single superior appoggiatura gradually took more and more time value from the main note, until it occupied about half the time of the main note. This interpretation—letting the appoggiatura take about half the time of the main note[42]—seems generally applicable to the first and third forms shown above, but not to the second, the *coulé* or so-called passing appoggiatura, which should take its time value from the *preceding* note. Quantz states that to perform the *durchgehende Vorschläge* (passing appoggiatura) this way is a part of French style; Edward Reilly conjectures that Quantz's insistence on this interpretation may have been occasioned by the performances he heard in Paris in 1726 and 1727.[43] Quantz gives the following example of the passing appoggiatura:[44]

Example 10

In a later chapter of the *Versuch*, another example of this ornament:

Example 11

is accompanied by the statement that "The little notes belong in the time of the notes preceding them, and hence must not, as in the second example, fall in the time of those that follow them."[45] Quantz's "second example" is as follows.

Example 12

The realization of the *coulé* in the time of the preceding note is supported by several French sources as well as by Quantz. For instance, Jean Rousseau, in his *Traité de la viole* of 1687, gives the following example of a *coulé*.[46]

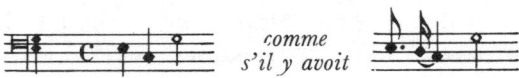

Example 13

Jean-Jacques Rousseau gives this example of the *coulé* in his *Dictionnaire*, the original edition of which appeared about 1768:[47]

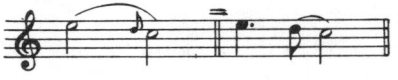

Example 14

Most eighteenth-century French sources give no clues as to the correct rhythmic interpretation of the *coulé*; those that do, apart from keyboard treatises,[48] agree that it should be performed in the time of the preceding note.[49]

Apart from the information to be found in the theoretical sources, an examination of Leclair's music by itself suggests that the *coulé* was generally performed before the beat. In numerous instances, if the *coulé* were executed in the time of the following note, awkward associations such as parallel ninths would result, as in the following examples.

Opus 5, Sonata 1, *Adagio*, measure 13

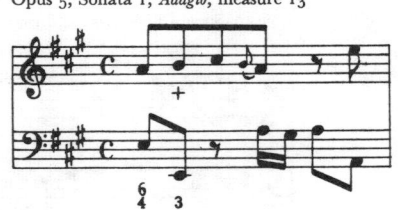

Example 15a

xvii

Example 15b

Example 17

Significantly, relations of this kind never occur when the *coulé* is executed in the time of the preceding note. Particularly in the first three books, this interpretation seems uniformly preferable to any other.

In the second half of the eighteenth century, the *coulé* gradually came to be performed in the time of the following note. The earliest reference Aldrich finds to this later interpretation of the *coulé* is in a letter Rameau wrote to d'Alembert in 1760.[50] Leclair's fourth book, written about 1738, contains several passages in which the *coulé* should probably be performed in the time of the following note. In nearly every such case the *coulés* concerned occur not singly but as members of a longer ornamental phrase, and the individual *coulé* is not slurred to the note that immediately follows it. Perhaps the use of the term *coulé* is inappropriate here, since the slur is a fundamental property of the ornament to which the term correctly applies.[51]

In some instances of the form of the *coulé* under discussion, the small notes descending stepwise occur in close conjunction with ornamental notes that are played on the beat, and it seems likely that the small notes may also occur on the beat, as at the asterisks in Example 16.

Performance of the small notes on the beat seems appropriate to Example 17 as well, despite Quantz's contrary advice for the similar examples on page xvii, above.

The *conjunct multiple appoggiatura* appears in the Leclair sonatas as a group of from two to eleven small notes. These ornamental notes were apparently treated with the greatest freedom; most sources do not even state whether they should be performed in the time of the preceding note, the following note, or both. In the Leclair sonatas they should usually be performed, I think, in the time of the preceding note, as in Example 18.

Example 18

Aldrich presents separate chapters on the *superior oscillation* (the trill) and the *inferior oscillation* (the mordent). Leclair indicates ornaments of both types with a small cross (+), and only from the context can the performer determine the execution. Although *tremblement* is perhaps the most common French term for the trill, *cadence* is also used frequently; most cadence groups were accompanied by this ornament, and the term *cadence* became transferred to the ornament itself. All superior oscillations, in whatever form, begin with the upper auxiliary.[52] Aldrich lists three basic melodic forms:

1. The *tremblement simple*, consisting of only the main note and its upper neighbor:

Example 19

Leclair uses no special sign to indicate this trill. Presumably it is to be performed where no other kind is specified.

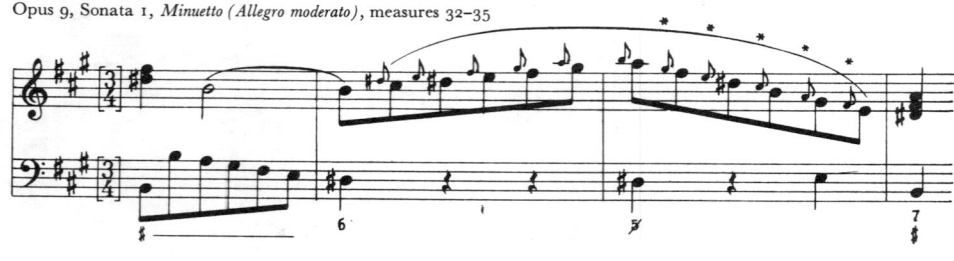

Example 16

2. The *tremblement fermé* or *tremblement avec une liaison*, which ends with an anticipation of the following note:

Example 20

Leclair usually indicates this type of trill by writing in the anticipation as a regular eighth or sixteenth note:

Example 21

3. The *tremblement et pincé* ends with a descent to the degree below the main note, followed by a return to the main note:

Example 22

Leclair specifies this ornament by writing out the last two notes, either as small notes or as regular notes:

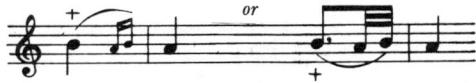

Example 23

In the latter case the time values used are not intended to suggest actual performance; the two notes should continue the speed of the trill itself, which may or may not coincide with the written value of the notes. Aldrich conjectures that the *tremblement et pincé* should probably be used in more places than Leclair specifies.[53]

In each of its melodic forms, the trill may be performed many different ways rhythmically. Aldrich lists several, some of which seem applicable to the Leclair sonatas. In the *cadence avec un appuy* (or *cadence appuyée*), the first note, the upper auxiliary, is held for some time before the oscillation begins. In Leclair's time the *appuy* was usually held for about half the duration of the trill:

Example 24

Aldrich also mentions a type of *cadence appuyée* called the *tremblement etouffé*, in which the *appuy* is held for almost the whole value of the main note.[54]

Leclair usually designates the *cadence appuyée* with a small note preceding the ornament itself:

Example 25

Among the possible interpretations of the *cadence appuyée*, the most common is the *tremblement lié*, in which the *appuy* is not repeated at the beginning of the oscillation:

Example 26

In the music of some French composers the *appuy* is occasionally expressed by an ordinary note whose time value approximates the actual duration of the *appuy*. When a trilled note is preceded by a note one degree higher in pitch and joined to it with a slur, the first note is a written-out *appuy*, and the trill should be performed as a *tremblement lié*.[55] This type of trill is described by Corrette in one of his violin treatises ("The cadence is always prepared by the note above [i.e., the upper appoggiatura] and is denoted by a t. or +.") and illustrated with the following example:[56]

Example 27

The difference between Corrette's example and Leclair's usual practice is that Corrette writes the *appuy* as a regular note but Leclair expresses it with a small note.

In movements of a slow or moderate tempo the *cadence appuyée* is particularly expressive, and it is unfortunate that comparatively few present-day violinists perform it correctly. Consider, for instance, the closing cadence of the first movement of Sonata 4 in the fourth book; the following example shows (a) Leclair's notation, (b) an interpretation without a sustained *appuy,* and (c) an interpretation with a sustained *appuy.* It is obvious, I think, that version (c) is musically more effective than version (b).[57]

Opus 9, Sonata 4, *Andante Spirituoso,* measures 75–77

Example 28

In contrast with the *cadence appuyée,* the *cadence jetée,* also called the *tremblement subit* or *cadence sans appuy,* begins directly with an oscillation in equal note values. Leclair has no special way of indicating this ornament; it probably occurs when the embellished note stands by itself, with no slur or preceding *appuy,* and particularly in joyous or vivacious movements.

In eighteenth-century usage the oscillation of a *tremblement* was often stopped on the main note before the full time of the note had elapsed, and the time was filled out by holding the main note, creating the *cadence coupée.*

Example 29

Montéclair gives a particularly clear explanation of this type of trill:

> When the trill prepares a cadence (which is a "relaxation" or a "resting place" of the melody) it [the trill] must be sustained, then executed slowly and evenly. To sustain a trill is to put down the finger which must trill, keep it immobile for half a bow stroke, trill on the other half, and to raise it, after having trilled, a moment before the stroke is finished, so one can distinguish the note on which the trill is written [the main note].[58]

The trill described by Montéclair is actually both *appuyée* and *coupée.* In the Leclair sonatas the *cadence coupée* may occur on a trill whether or not the trill has an *appuy.* The use of the *cadence coupée* depends solely on the sense of the musical phrase, since there is never any indication for its use.

Jean Rousseau gives a lengthy and complex set of rules as to when the *cadence avec un appuy* and *cadence sans appuy* should occur.[59] The list is summarized in Putnam Aldrich's dissertation.[60]

Aldrich mentions another kind of trill called the *cadence à progression,* in which the speed of the oscillation gradually increases.[61] He feels that it was probably used more frequently than specific mention of it in eighteenth-century sources suggests.[62]

Example 30

In the Leclair sonatas, this realization seems particularly appropriate to the performance of a trill that is prolonged over several beats or even several measures (for example, measure 53 of the *Allegro* of Sonata 3 in the fourth book).

Of necessity, each of the illustrations above has shown a particular number of oscillations; most sources say nothing, however, about the number of oscillations in a trill.[63] Obviously, a trill should be performed faster than the predominant rhythmic motion of the movement in which it appears, or it will lose its ornamental function. But too many present-day violinists seem to think that trills are to be played as fast as the performer can alternate the two notes in question. Trills played thus may sound brilliant, but they can hardly be melodically expressive.

The tempo of a movement should help determine the choice of a speed for any given trill. When the trill occurs on a short note-value in a fast movement, a rapid oscillation is inevitable; when trills occur on long notes and in slow movements, however, the performer may have a wide choice of speeds, and his *bon goût* must govern the selection of one which is musically appropriate.

The *inferior oscillation beginning with the main note* is variously called the *pincé, pincement, martellement,* or *battement.* Aldrich explains the early history of this ornament and includes varying descriptions by Mersenne and Jean Rousseau.[64] As performed on bowed instruments the *pincé* usually included only two or three oscillations, occurred on the beat, and was played rather quickly.[65]

Example 31

Corrette gives the following example of the *pincé* in his treatise of 1738:[66]

Example 32

In a later treatise on the violin Corrette presents a different rhythmic interpretation of the same ornament:[67]

Example 33

As these examples show, the performer has considerable freedom in choosing the speed of the oscillation.

Leclair indicates the *pincé* with the small cross (+), as did many of the viol composers. Aldrich finds that eighteenth-century sources give little precise information about the proper application of the *pincé*, but he does present a list of general rules. The *pincé* is generally to be performed:

1. On the upper note of a semitone in the scale.
2. On a melody note that is approached from below.
3. On a long note that is preceded by a short note.
4. On a strong beat, when the movement is comparatively slow, or on the strong subdivision of a beat when the movement is in rapid note values.
5. On the first note of a piece or of a phrase, if the movement is not too rapid. The *pincé*, in this position, must stop on the main note for the duration of the second half of its time value.
6. The *pincé* should never be introduced upon two notes in succession.[68]

Aldrich immediately adds that the performance of a *pincé* on a given note depends on how many of these rules the note fulfils, and states that if only two of the rules apply, the ornament should not be introduced. He uses the following musical example to clarify these rules:[69]

Example 34

Aldrich asserts that the *pincé* must be introduced at points *a* and *d*, where the first four rules apply, that it may be introduced at *b* and *e*, where three of the first four rules apply, and that it must not be introduced at *c* or *f*, where only two of the rules apply.

In Leclair's music it seems logical to use a *pincé* on notes which carry the small cross and which conform to these rules, but to use a *tremblement* on crossed notes that do not conform. Since the same sign is used to designate both *pincé* and *tremblement*, in many situations only *le bon goût* of the performer can decide which ornament is suitable.

As Aldrich points out, his first rule implies that within the scale the *pincé* is appropriate to the tonic and subdominant notes, and the *tremblement* to the supertonic, mediant, and leading tones. Aldrich's second rule seems to have the most importance of the six for Leclair's sonatas: in ascending melodies the *pincé* frequently seems much more natural than the *tremblement*, and, conversely, in descending melodies the *tremblement* often seems more appropriate. Aldrich cites only one source for his sixth rule—that the *pincé* should never be introduced upon two notes in succession—and I have found no other source that mentions it. Furthermore, the rule creates a problem in the interpretation of a passage in which several successive notes carry the small cross. Several authors declare that the *tremblement* is not appropriate in such a situation; Corrette, for instance, states: "One can make trills on all the notes, but one never performs three of them in succession."[70] The use of several consecutive *pincés* is common in clavecin music of the French baroque,[71] and I believe that there are situations in the Leclair sonatas as well where a *pincé* might be used to good effect on several successive notes carrying the +, as in measures 26 and 27 of Example 35.

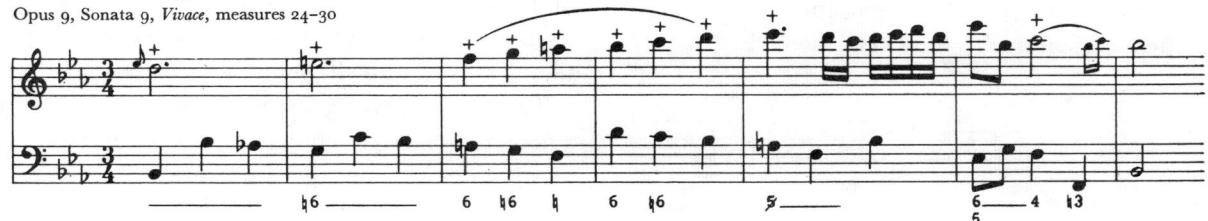

Example 35

The *inferior oscillation beginning with the auxiliary* has no special name in French sources. Aldrich says that it was "regarded as a compound ornament which had no individuality of its own but consisted of an inferior appoggiatura *plus* an inferior oscillation."[72] The ornament bears the composite name *port de voix et pincé,* and the *clavecin* composers often indicate it by combining the sign for the *port de voix* with the sign for the *pincé*. In vocal music the ornament is indicated in the same manner as the single *port de voix,* with a small note.

Example 36

The performer thus faces the problem of deciding when this mark designates a simple *port de voix* and when it calls for a *port de voix* with one or more inferior oscillations. Aldrich points out that many authorities discuss the *port de voix* with no mention of any sort of oscillation, while others state that the ornament always ends with an oscillation.[73] Jean-Jacques Rousseau's illustration of the *port de voix* in his *Dictionnaire* includes an oscillation:[74]

Example 37

In his *Traité de la viole* Jean Rousseau writes, "The *martellement* [*i.e.,* the inferior oscillation] is always inseparable from the *port de voix,* since the *port de voix* must always be terminated by a *martellement.*"[75] Aldrich conjectures that the oscillation became rather commonly associated with the *port de voix* in the early years of the eighteenth century, and that the two were associated as a rule rather than as an exception by the middle of the century.

Like the single *port de voix,* the *port de voix et pincé* yields itself to several different rhythmic interpretations. Aldrich gives several examples, showing the appoggiatura as performed in the time of the preceding note, of the main note, and of both preceding and main notes. In my opinion, the following realizations are the most suitable to the Leclair sonatas:

Example 38

Both include only one oscillation, but when the main note is unusually long a greater number of oscillations may be appropriate.

In the Leclair sonatas, where to use the *port de voix et pincé* must be decided by the performer. The use of the *pincé* with almost any *port de voix* cannot be considered "wrong," but its "rightness" depends on the character of the piece and the length of the main note.

In summary: Leclair indicates appoggiaturas—both single and multiple, from above and below—with small notes. Most single appoggiaturas are played on the beat except the *coulé,* which occurs in the time of the preceding note. The *tremblement* and the *pincé* are both indicated by the small cross, and the performer must determine from the context of the note which ornament is the more suitable, and which of its various rhythmic and melodic forms is best.

I have attempted to supply a basic fund of information for the interpretation of Leclair's ornaments. Within this context a performer is free to choose from among a number of equally "correct" methods of performance; I recognize that in the twentieth century, as in the eighteenth, a happy solution to every problem of musical interpretation depends on no set of rules so much as on the *bon goût* of the performer. In playing Leclair's sonatas the violinist has the opportunity, indeed the responsibility, to make independent judgments in the light of his own musical taste.

Bowing

Leclair's bowing practice is one of the most important elements of his style. Three bowing indications appear in his works, the slur, the vertical stroke, and the dot. Interpreting the slur is a fairly simple task. When a number of notes are joined by a slur and no other signs are present, the notes are usually played legato, and always in one bow-stroke. A problem does arise, however, in the fourth book, where a mark that appears to be a slur may actually be an indication of phrasing. Long phrase marks are rare in the earlier books but quite common in the fourth book.

The interpretation of both the stroke and the dot is difficult; historically the signs have rather similar meanings, and eighteenth-century theorists give inconsistent, if not actually conflicting, discussions of them.[76] To find interpretations that make sense for the Leclair sonatas, one must first take note of the musical context of each mark, then match the situation against the eighteenth-century sources to arrive at a rendition that is historically sound and musically effective.

The vertical stroke, written above (or occasionally below) a note, is found frequently in Leclair's third and fourth books, mostly in movements of a moderate or fast tempo. The speed of the notes that carry it varies greatly, from quarter notes in a *Largo* movement (Book IV, Sonata 3, *Sarabande*) to sixteenth notes in a *Presto* (Book IV, Sonata 3, *Tambourin*). It appears in both violin and continuo parts. Several notes in succession may bear strokes, especially in fast movements. The stroke is almost never found on notes that are slurred together (e.g., [notation]),[77] although in a few movements the stroke appears over the last note in a slurred group (e.g., [notation]).

A discussion of possible interpretations of the stroke requires the mention of an important problem of terminology: eighteenth-century sources suggest almost no difference between the terms *staccato* and *spiccato*. Brossard defines staccato as ". . . nearly the same thing as spiccato. That is to say that the stringed instruments ought to make all their strokes dry, without connection, and well detached or separated from each other"; spiccato is described as ". . . to separate, to make disjunct. . . . it is necessary to make the sounds very detached or separated. . . . it is almost the same as staccato."[78] One of Corrette's violin treatises contains an alphabetical index of musical terms, in which Corrette writes under a single heading: "Staccato or Spiccato means that the bow strokes should be played in a dry manner, without dragging, and very detached."[79] These definitions are typical; they show clearly how closely the terms staccato and spiccato were related in the eighteenth century.

Most eighteenth-century sources state that the stroke indicates a type of separation, staccato or *détaché*, but the degree and manner of separation varies considerably. Leopold Mozart states:

A composer often writes notes which he wishes to be played each with a strongly accented stroke and separated one from another. In such cases he signifies the kind of bowing by means of little strokes which he writes over or under the notes.[80]

Most of Mozart's examples of the stroke show it used on a group of slurred notes; in that situation, Mozart says, the notes should be "detached in one up stroke separating each by means of a short pressure."[81]

Quantz states that "in playing the notes above which little strokes appear, the bow must be detached a little from the strings."[82] He immediately qualifies this clear interpretation of the stroke, as follows:

This [detaching the bow from the strings] means only those notes in which the time permits. Thus the quavers in the Allegro, and the semiquavers in the Allegretto are excepted if many follow one another; they must be played with a very short bow-stroke, but the bow must never be detached or removed from the strings. If it were always raised as high as is required when we say that it is detached, there would not be enough time to return it to the string at the proper time, and notes of this kind would sound as if they were chopped or whipped.[83]

Quantz's point is important to the performance of the Leclair sonatas: when one is playing notes that bear strokes, the bow may or may not leave the string. Geminiani's definition of the stroke as "a Staccato, where the Bow is taken off the Strings at every Note"[84] is misleading, since Geminiani had a narrow view of the use of staccato bowing. He approved of its application to quarter notes at a slow tempo or to eighth notes at a fast tempo, but he strongly disapproved of its use on eighth notes at a slow tempo or sixteenth notes at a fast tempo.[85] Other sources suggest that the staccato was used much more widely and freely than Geminiani's comments imply.

In movements of a slow or moderate tempo the stroke usually indicates a sharp separation, followed by a silence of articulation that assumes approximately half the value of the note. The practice is described in the article on *détaché* in Rousseau's dictionary: "Type of execution in which, instead of holding notes for their entire value, one separates them by rests, [whose time-value is] taken from each note."[86]

Quantz is even more explicit. Speaking of notes which bear strokes, he says:

In notes of this kind you must be regulated by whether the tempo of the piece is very slow or very quick, and must not shorten notes in the Adagio as much as those in the Allegro; otherwise those in the Adagio will sound all too dry and meagre. The general rule that may be established in this regard is as follows: if little strokes stand above several notes, they must sound half as long as their true value. But if a little stroke stands above only one note, after which several of lesser value follow, it indicates not only that the note must be played half as long, but also that it must at the same time be accented with a pressure of the bow.[87]

A stroke appearing over a succession of very quick notes lends itself to two interpretations: a staccato in which the bow does not leave the string, or a spiccato which utilizes a bounding bow. For example, the *Allegro ma non troppo* in Sonata 6, Book III, frequently alternates [notation] and [notation]. A spiccato interpretation of the latter group seems appropriate; even though there is no slur over the group, the three notes do not necessarily demand three separate bow-strokes. Quantz presents two examples in which successive notes bearing strokes should be played in a single up-bow; he feels that this bowing is especially desirable in passages of widely separated notes.[88] Parenthetically he adds, "This manner of playing is also much less tiring than playing each note with a separate stroke."[89]

Since the stroke suggests a strongly accented bowing, the possibility of *martelé* bowing arises; indeed, in various of Leclair's sonatas the vertical stroke occasionally resembles the modern sign for *martelé*. This interpretation is unlikely, however, for two reasons: the construction of the mid-eighteenth-century bow renders it almost incapable of *martelé* bowing, and there are few if any places in Leclair's sonatas where the bowing seems musically appropriate.

To conclude this discussion of the vertical stroke, I refer the reader to a particularly vivid illustration of the fact that the mark had no single meaning in eighteenth-century violin music: in his treatise on violin playing, Leopold Mozart shows by means of several musical examples that even with one small melodic figure the stroke can have different interpretations.[90]

In Leclair's third book dots are used sparingly, but they appear frequently in the fourth book. There they are found

xxiii

only in movements of a moderate or fast tempo, and almost exclusively in the violin part. Successive notes bearing dots are nearly always joined by a slur; Leclair includes under one slur as many as fifteen notes with dots. Groups of notes with dots but without a slur are found only rarely.[91] Mozart explains the dot as follows:

It happens also that under the circle [i.e., the slur] . . . dots are written under or over the notes. This signifies that the notes lying within the slur are not only to be played in one [presumably up-] bow-stroke, but must be separated from each other by a slight pressure of the bow.[92]

Quantz offers a remarkably clear explanation of the dot:

If dots stand above the notes they must be articulated or attacked with a short bow, but must not be detached. If a slur is added above the dots, all the notes within it must be taken in one bow-stroke and stressed with a pressure of the bow.[93]

Corrette similarly states that notes which bear dots and are written under a slur should be performed as "equal notes, articulated with a single bow stroke."[94]

Perhaps the most obvious interpretation of the dot as it appears in the Leclair sonatas is a light staccato on the string, but I believe that another reading of a series of slurred notes bearing dots is perfectly possible: a stroke consisting entirely of lifted notes. This interpretation, the *staccato volante*, is not specifically described in eighteenth-century sources, but Mozart speaks of a bowing technique which closely approximates it: ". . . you must also learn to detach many notes in one stroke . . . separating them by a quick lift of the bow."[95] He illustrates this bowing with an example in which twelve sixteenth notes are grouped under one bow. The *staccato volante* seems quite appropriate in passages such as that in Sonata 1 of the fourth book, *Allegro assai*, measures 20–21.

Several sources give direct comparisons of the dot and the stroke. Mondonville's collection *Les Sons Harmoniques* (c. 1738) presents a musical example in which the dot represents *articulation* while the stroke represents *détaché*.[96]

Perhaps the clearest distinction between these two bowing indications is presented by Quantz:

For just as a distinction is to be made between strokes and dots without slurs above them, that is, the notes with strokes must be played with completely detached strokes, and those with dots simply with short strokes and in a sustained manner, so a similar distinction is required when there are slurs above the notes.[97]

From the preceding discussion it should be apparent that no single interpretation can be prescribed for either the stroke or the dot, yet one broad statement can be made about the difference between them: whether or not slurs are involved, the stroke nearly always indicates greater separation than the dot. This principle, stated or implied by several theorists, is in my opinion a reliable guide to the bowing of the Leclair sonatas.

A final bowing problem is that after indicating the start of a particular bowing, Leclair frequently neglects to make clear how long it should continue. For example, a short pattern recurring sequentially may be marked with strokes in its original statement and not in the succeeding ones; the performer must decide whether the staccato bowing should be used in all statements of the pattern. Occasionally an ambiguity of this sort persists through an entire movement; Leclair may mark the first few measures with dots or strokes, and again the performer must decide whether the marks should be observed throughout the movement.[98] Quantz offers the following advice:

Note here in passing that if many figures of the same sort follow one another, and the bowing of only the first is indicated, the others must be played in the same manner as long as no other species of notes appears. The same is true of notes with strokes above them. If, for example, only two, three, or four are marked with strokes, the following notes of the same species and value are also played staccato. If they are not, the desired effect will not be produced, and perfect uniformity of expression will never be achieved.[99]

These comments are pertinent to the Leclair sonatas, and the present-day violinist should have them well in mind as he determines the details of bowing for each sonata.

Editorial Practice

Original editions of Leclair's third and fourth books of sonatas, now owned by the University of Michigan library, and a copy of the posthumous sonata owned by the Royal Conservatory of Music in Brussels are the sources of the present edition. My aim in preparing these volumes has been to present a faithful picture of the sonatas as Leclair left them, in a format useful to both the scholar and the performer.

Many modern editions clarify all the ambiguities of the source and solve all the notational problems, thus denying the performer the opportunity to see what the composer wrote and to interpret it according to his own judgment. To avoid this state of affairs I have, in the first place, retained all of Leclair's performance suggestions in my edition. The violinist will find it necessary to add a number of dynamics, phrasing, and bowings, yet he may do so with the knowledge that the marks which appear in the edition, apart from those in square brackets, are Leclair's, not the editor's.

I have avoided making arbitrary interpretations of Leclair wherever a choice of legitimate readings exists. For example, I have left passages marked "arpeggio" in their original form, rather than write out the arpeggio, so each violinist will be free to interpret Leclair's mark as he chooses.

A serious problem that attended the making of this edition was the inconsistency of certain usages in the sources. For example, in the seventh sonata of the fourth book, written for alternate performance on the transverse flute, the instrument is referred to as "flute," "fluto," and "flauto." This particular case is not musically significant, of course, but when accidentals and other elements of notation are treated similarly the inconsistency can be highly confusing. Occasionally a whole passage may be written one way in one section of the movement and a slightly different way later on; this does not necessarily mean that the passage should be played two ways. In the edition I have noted a number of important inconsistencies; the violinist must decide for himself how to resolve them.

My alterations of the sources are of two kinds: mere modernizations of Leclair's notation, and genuine editorial additions, clarifications, or interpretations. Changes of the first sort are unmarked, since they affect merely the appearance, not the interpretation, of the music; other changes are enclosed in square brackets or footnoted, to show clearly the condition of the source without the editorial alteration.

To make Leclair's notation intelligible to the modern performer, I have altered accidentals and key signatures to conform with present-day convention, corrected the spelling of musical terms and the titles of movements, indicated first and second endings by the conventional means, and imposed modern usage on the accidentals governing the bass figures. In a few instances of the appearance of *segue* next to a figuration in the violin part, I have written out the pattern in the succeeding measures; but where there is the slightest doubt how a *segue* pattern should be repeated I have retained the original notation so the violinist can choose what he considers an appropriate rendering.

In an effort to improve the readability of the often cluttered notation of the violin part, I have occasionally combined notes on a single stem and eliminated superfluous rests; I have avoided pursuing any rigorous policy of rest-use and stem-use, however, to preserve the sense of any subtleties of musical structure which Leclair's own use of stems and rests may have been intended to convey.

Bracketed editorial accidentals have been added to the edition to clarify Leclair's notation. Time signatures are shown in their original form, together with their modern equivalents in brackets. The small cross specifying a trill occasionally carries a bracketed accidental indicating that the upper note of the trill should be altered chromatically. Where Leclair writes incomplete measures I have added bracketed time signatures to clarify the metrical structure of the passage; for example, Leclair's c ♩♩♩♩|♩♩|♩♩♩♩ is written c ♩♩♩♩| [2/4] ♩♩| [C] ♩♩♩♩ in the edition. Changes in Leclair's figuring of the bass are bracketed or footnoted.

Leclair nearly always places his dynamic marks between the violin and continuo staves, and I have assumed that the marks apply to both parts. In a few instances a dynamic marking appears over the violin part in a musical context which suggests that the mark is intended for the violin alone, but, more often than not, those of Leclair's dynamic marks that appear over the violin part were placed there simply because there is insufficient space between the violin and continuo lines. The fingerings that appear in a few sonatas are all the composer's. *Tasto solo* indications in the continuo occur mostly over held notes;[100] although I have, of course, retained Leclair's ties, the keyboard performer may wish to ignore some of them and repeat the bass note, particularly if the continuo line is not being doubled by a cello or a viola da gamba. The performer may also elect to double a *tasto solo* at the octave.[101] Strokes and dots for the continuo line have been placed nearly always above the line, to prevent their colliding with the figures for the bass.

In realizing the figured bass, I have tried to avoid doubling the violin line at the unison or octave, which would weaken the independence of the violin line; to keep the realization for the most part under the violin line; and to avoid detracting from the interest of the violin line. Performers who find my realizations too simple may readily write or improvise more elaborate ones, since Leclair's figures are faithfully reproduced in the edition. Although my realizations normally proceed in three voices, I have added an extra voice where the context seems to demand it, and conversely I have dropped a voice where the continuo line moves into an unusually high range, or where retaining the original number of voices would produce awkward doublings.

I have standardized, according to modern convention, the source's frequently eccentric notation of rhythm. Within a single sonata, triplet sixteenths may be written ♪♪♪ in one place and ♪♪♪ in another (with or without the triplet designation). Throughout the sonatas, particularly in slow movements, occur rhythmic groups which are "incorrect" by modern standards (*e.g.*, the equivalent of ten sixteenth notes in the time of a half note). Dotted rhythms frequently may seem "wrong," since the value of the dot was variable in baroque music. In resolving these and similar difficulties, I have given each original reading in a footnote, so the performer can readily make his own interpretation of the source if he should so desire. Several of Leclair's slow movements contain ornamental flourishes which doubtless are not intended to be performed within a strict metrical framework, such as the opening movement of Sonata 12 in the third book. The performer should feel free to exercise considerable freedom in the rhythmic interpretation of such ornamental passages.

Two doctoral dissertations that bear directly on the performance of eighteenth-century music should be consulted by anyone who wishes to gain added insight into the problems of performing Leclair's sonatas. Newman Powell discusses rhythmic problems of various sorts and presents an excellent discussion of the problem of *notes inégales*.[102] Barbara Seagrave deals with violin music earlier than the Leclair sonatas, but her discussion of the bowing of certain dances is decidedly pertinent to the performance of these dances as they occur in the music of this edition.[103]

I wish to express my thanks to the University Council on Research at Tulane University for a grant which aided substantially in the publication of this edition. Special thanks should also go to Dr. Putnam Aldrich, who read the entire section concerning ornaments, above, and offered valuable suggestions, and to Dr. Barbara Seagrave, who thoughtfully loaned me several microfilms and helped me solve a number of bowing problems. Finally, I am pleased to acknowledge the large debt I owe my wife, who, in addition to proofreading all the sonatas, has otherwise given freely of her time and energies. She has consistently and patiently offered not only encouragement but also musical assistance; in particular I am grateful for her numerous suggestions for the improvement of the continuo realizations.

Robert E. Preston
Newcomb College
Tulane University

Notes

[1] Lionel de La Laurencie, *L'École française de violon de Lully à Viotti; études d'histoire et d'esthétique* (3 vols.; Paris: Delagrave, 1922-24), I, 269-314.

[2] Marc Pincherle, *Jean-Marie Leclair l'aîné* (Paris: La Colombe, 1952), 17-50.

[3] One of his younger brothers, born September 23, 1703, was also named Jean-Marie, and also became a composer, usually signing his name "J.-M. Leclair le second."

[4] Johann Joachim Quantz, "Herrn Johann Joachim Quantzens Lebenslauf von ihm selbst entworfen," in Friedrich Wilhelm Marpurg, *Historisch-kritische Beyträge zur Aufnahme der Musik* (5 vols.; Berlin: J. J. Schüssens sel. Wittwe, 1754), I, 236.

[5] *Mercure de France* (April 17 and 19, 1728), 856.

[6] In his *Essai sur la musique ancienne et moderne* (4 vols.; Paris: Ph.-D. Pierres, 1780), III, 405, Jean Benjamin de La Borde claims that the bass part of Leclair's Opus 1 was actually written by Cheron, but this contention is not supported by any other source.

[7] Marpurg, *Historisch-kritische Beyträge*, I, 466-467.

[8] La Laurencie, *L'École française de violon*, I, 240-242.

[9] Arend Koole, in his *Leven en Werken van Pietro Locatelli da Bergamo* (Amsterdam: Jasonspers, Universiteitspers, 1949), 46-48, summarizes the known facts bearing on possible meetings between Leclair and Locatelli.

[10] Pincherle, *Jean-Marie Leclair l'aîné*, 43: ". . . retiré, sinistre au point d'inspirer à l'entourage de Leclair les plus vives appréhensions."

[11] La Laurencie, *L'École française de violon*, I, 299-302.

[12] A trio sonata published in Paris in 1711. See La Laurencie, *L'École française de violon*, I, 77-78.

[13] Michel Corrette, *Le Maitre de clavecin pour l'accompagnement, methode theorique et pratique* . . . (Paris: 1753), Preface, p. A (throughout these notes, all eighteenth-century quotations and titles will retain their original spelling, capitalization, and accents):

Ce fut à ce Concert où parû pour la premiere fois les Trio de *Corelli* imprimé à Rome. Cette Musique d'un genre nouveau encouragea tous les Auteurs à travailler dans un gout plus brillant. tel fut le Caprice de Mr. *Rebel* le pere, tous les Concerts prirent une autre forme: Les Scènes et les Symphonies d'Opéra cederent la présence aux Sonates. . . .

[14] *Ibid.*, Preface, p. B:

Dans le même tems *Corelli* donna son 5e. Oeuvre, Chef d'Oeuvre de l'art. Feu Monsieur le Duc d'Orleans depuis Régent du Royaume étant extremement Curieux de Musique voulut entendre ces Sonates mais ne pouvant trouver alors aucun Violon dans Paris Capable de joüer par accords il fut obligé de les faire chanter par trois voix. Mais cette sterilité de Violon ne dura pas longlems [sic]. Chacun travailla jour et nuit a apprendre ces Sonates; desorte qu'au bout de quelques années parut trois Violons qui les executerent. *Chatillon* qui étoit aussi Organiste *Duval* et *Baptiste*. Ce dernier fut exprès à Rome pour les entendre joüer par l'Auteur.

On peut juger par la quantité de bons Violons qu'il y a présentement à Paris, combien la Musique à fait de progrès depuis l'invention de la Sonate, car les Symphonies d'Opera n'auroient jamais formé de si grands sujets.

[15] Corrette's words "de les faire chanter par trois voix" could perhaps be translated quite differently: "to have them played by three violins." This translation would seem more in keeping with the musical quality of the Corelli works, a vocal performance of which is rather difficult to imagine. I think it preferable, however, to give the words "chanter" and "voix" a literal interpretation, as I have done in the body of the text.

[16] Pincherle, *Jean-Marie Leclair l'aîné*, 14.

[17] La Laurencie gives a detailed history of the violin sonata in France prior to Leclair in the first four chapters of *L'École française de violon*, I, 1-268. Also, William S. Newman devotes two chapters in his excellent study of the baroque sonata to the development of the sonata in France. See *The Sonata in the Baroque Era* (revised edition; Chapel Hill: University of North Carolina Press, 1966), 351-392.

[18] Analyses of the Leclair sonatas and a discussion of their style may be found in my study "The Sonatas for Violin and Figured Bass by Jean-Marie Leclair l'aîné" (2 vols.; unpublished dissertation, University of Michigan, 1959).

[19] TROISIEME LIVRE / DE / SONATES / A VIOLON SEUL / avec la Basse Continüe. / Composées / PAR Mr. LECLAIR L'AINÉ / Ordinaire de la Musique de la Chapelle / Et de la Chambre du Roy. / Gravées par Mme. Leclair son Epouse. / DEDIÉES / AU ROY. / OEUVRE V. / Prix en blanc 12tt. / A PARIS / Chez L'auteur, rue St. Benoist proche la porte de l'Abaïe St. Germain. / La Ve. Boivin, rue St. honoré à la Régle D'or. / Le Sr. Leclerc, rue du Roule à la Croix D'or. / Avec Privilége du Roy.

[20] This rather implausible bit of flattery must refer to Louis XV's involvement in the War of the Polish Succession, 1733-35.

[21] Sire,

La grâce que Vôtre Majesté vient de me faire authorise l'homage que j'ose luy rendre; pour la première fois, j'aporte à ses pieds les fruits d'une muse domestique. Que ce titre est glorieux pour moy! Le désir ardent de le mériter un jour a soutenu ma foiblesse contre les difficultés d'un art long et pénible; le bonheur du succez a comblé mon ambition. Le travail de toute ma vie est trop payé par les moments que Votre Majesté a daigné prêter l'oreille à mes sons. Ces moments toujours précieux le sont encore plus dans la conjoncture présente, mais, peu-être Votre Majesté se souvient-elle que le tems des conquêtes du feu Roy fut celuy des plus grands progrès de nôtre art. La gloire du Souverain influe sur le génie des sujets; il est naturel qu'une nation qui vous est soumise ne cède à aucun peuple pour les talens agréables, non plus que pour les talens utiles ou nécessaires. Je suis avec le plus profond respect, Sire, de Vôtre Majesté, le très humble, très obéissant et très fidelle sujet et serviteur.

J.-M. Leclair, l'aîné.

[22] QUATRIEME LIVRE / DE / SONATES / A VIOLON SEUL / avec la Basse Continue. / Composées, / PAR Mr LE CLAIR L'AINÉ / Gravées par Mme. Le Clair son Epouse. / Dediées, / A Son Altesse Royale / MADAME LA PRINCESSE / D'ORANGE / OEUVRE IX. / Prix en blanc 15tt. / A PARIS, / Chez l'auteur, ruë St. Benoist proche la

porte de l'Abaïe St. Germain. / Mme. La Ve. Boivin, ruë St. Honoré à la Régle D'or. / Le Sr. Le clerc, ruë du Roule à la Croix D'or. / Avec Privilége du Roy.

[23]A Son Altesse Royale Madame / La Princesse d'Orange.
 Madame

Le gout de V. A. R. pour les vraiës beautés de la Musique, et la Connoissance profonde que vous avés des principes de cet Art, ne sont pas les seuls motifs qui m'ont inspiré la confiance de vous offrir cet ouvrage—je sçai que non-contente d'aimer tous les talens, vous faites gloire de les proteger. je l'ai éprouvé, Madame, pendant tout le tems que j'ai passé dans vôtre Cour, où vous m'aviés fait lhonneur de m'apeller. Les aplaudissements sont la récompense la plus flateuse dès Arts. le souvenir de ceux que j'ai reçus de V. A. R. est plus precieux pour moi, que celui de vos bienfaits. je ferai toute ma vie de nouveaux efforts pour les justifier.
 Je suis
 Madame
 Avec le plus respectueux attachement
 de Votre Altesse Royale

Le très humble et tres
obeissant Serviteur.
LE CLAIR l'ainé

[24]Tous ceux qui voudront parvenir à executer cet ouvrage dans le gout de l'Auteur doivent S'attacher à trouver le Caractére de chaque piéce, ainsi que le veritable mouvement et la qualité de son qui convient aux differents morceaux. un point important et sur lequel on ne peut trop insister, c'est d'éviter cette confusion de notes que l'on ajoute aux morceaux de chant et d'expression, et qui ne servent qu'ua [sic] les defigurer. Il n'est pas moins ridicule de changer les mouvements à deux rondeaux faits l'un pour l'autre, et de joüer plus vite le majeur que le mineur: à la bonne heure que l'on egaië le majeur par la façon de le jouer, mais cela se peut faire sans precipiter la mesure.

Jai, trop d'obligation aux connoisseurs et au public des louanges flatteuses dont ils m'honorent de puis si longtems pour avoir épargné ni mon tems ni mes soins afin de rendre cet ouvrage aussi instructif qu'agréable j'ose esperer qu'on ne trouvera pas mauvais que je vend ce livre 15 ℔. de même qu'on ne débitera plus à lavenir les precedents qu'au meme prix de 15 ℔. à cause des frais considerables que je suis obligé de faire pour retablir quantité de planches entierrement usées.
For a discussion of the translation of this passage see page xvi.

[25]For a discussion of this puzzling sonata see my article "Leclair's posthumous solo sonata—an enigma," *Recherches sur la musique française classique*, VII (1967), 154-163.

[26]SONATE / A / VIOLON SEUL / ET / Basse Continue. / Ouvrage Postume / DE / M. LECLAIR / L'AINÉ / Gravée par sa Veuve. / Prix 1 ℔. 16 ß. / A PARIS / Chez Mme. La Ve. Leclair, dans le large de la rue du Four St. Germain / dans la Mason [sic] de M. Chavagnac Me. Masson Entrepreneur. / Et aux Adresses Ordinaires de Musiques. / A LYON / M. Castaud [,] place de la Comedie. / AVEC PRIVILEGE DU ROY. / Imprimée par Maillet.

[27]A catalogue of Leclair's works through Opus 13 was included in Opus 13, following the title page and dedication. The catalogue which appears in Opus 15 was apparently printed from the same plate, with the two posthumous sonatas added. As it appeared in Opus 13 the catalogue showed a raise in price for the first three books of solo sonatas, from 12 pounds to 15 pounds, a raise which Leclair had attempted to justify earlier in the *Avertissement* to the fourth book of solo sonatas.

[28]J.-M. Leclair, *Premier Livre de Sonates. Oeuvre III*, ed. Alexandre Guilmant and Joseph Debroux, in *Les Maîtres violinistes de l'école française du XVIIIe siècle* (Paris: Max Eschig, c. 1907). "Oeuvre III" is incorrect; these sonatas constitute Leclair's Opus 1.

Jean-Marie Leclair l'aîné, *Zwölf Sonaten für Violine und Generalbass nebst einem Trio für Violine, Violoncell und Generalbass*, ed. Robert Eitner (Vol. XXVII of *Publikationen älterer praktischer und theoretischer Musikwerke*, Leipzig: Breitkopf und Härtel, 1903). Although it is not stated in the title, this collection comprises Leclair's Opus 2, the second book of sonatas for violin and continuo.

[29]For a more detailed discussion of Leclair's harmonic practice see my article "The treatment of harmony in the violin sonatas of Jean-Marie Leclair," *Recherches sur la musique française classique*, III (1963), 131-144.

[30]Arnold's fine study of thorough-bass contains a chapter titled "Varieties of figuring," in which there are more references to Leclair than to any other composer. See Frank T. Arnold, *The Art of Accompaniment from a Thorough-Bass, as Practised in the XVIIth and XVIIIth Centuries* (London: Oxford University Press, Humphrey Milford, 1931), 861-882. This important source was reprinted by Dover Publications in 1965. The reprint is identical with the original edition, except that it is in two volumes instead of one.

[31]In *The Art of Accompaniment from a Thorough-Bass*, 870, Arnold gives a list of occasions when a $^6_4$ chord seems preferable to a simple $^6_3$.

[32]Putnam Aldrich, "The Principal *Agréments* of the Seventeenth and Eighteenth Centuries: A Study in Musical Ornamentation" (Unpublished dissertation, Harvard University, 1942).

[33]In only one instance does Leclair use a sixteenth note for a small note, at measure 87 of the *Aria grazioso* of Sonata 3 in Opus 5.

[34]J. J. Quantz, *On Playing the Flute* (1752), trans. Edward Reilly (London: Faber and Faber, 1966), 136, 162-163, 299, 320-326, and 328-335. Reilly's splendid translation originally appeared as part of a doctoral dissertation, "Quantz's *Versuch einer Anweisung die Flöte traversiere zu spielen*: A Translation and Study" (2 vols.; unpublished dissertation, University of Michigan, 1958).

[35]See, for example, the article *"goût"* in Jean-Jacques Rousseau, *Dictionnaire de musique* [Original edition c. 1768] (2 vols. [XIV and XV] of *Oeuvres de J. J. Rousseau*, Paris: Werdet et Lequien, 1826), I, 336-339.

[36]Aldrich, "The Principal *Agréments*," xxxiii.

[37]*Ibid*.

[38]The original French is given in note 24, above.

[39]A somewhat different translation appears in Ruth Halle Rowen, *Early Chamber Music* (New York: King's Crown Press, 1949), 107: "An important point—which one cannot stress too much—is to avoid that confusion of notes which are added to vocal pieces and that confusion of expression; they serve only to distort the compositions."

[40]Je prie Messieurs les Executants, de ne point trouver mauvais que je les fasse resouvenir de l'Avertissement qui est a la tete de mon 4e. Livre de Sonates. j'ay oublié de dire que je n'entend point par le terme d'Allegro, un mouvement trop vite; c'est un mouvement Guay. ceux qui le pressent trop, surtout dans les morceaux de caractaire comme dans la plus part des Fugues a quatre Temps, rendent le chant Trivial, au lieu d'en conserver la Noblesse. cet avis ne regarde que les personnes qui peuvent en avoir besoin.

Opus 13 contains three of Leclair's solo sonatas arranged as trio sonatas, Sonata 12 from the first book and Sonatas 8 and 12 from the second book. Each contains a fugue in $\frac{4}{4}$, hence Leclair's admonition concerning the tempo of fugues. Two of the fugues in question have the tempo marking *Allegro ma non troppo*, yet in spite of the fact that the *Allegro* tempo is clearly qualified, Leclair was apparently concerned that these movements might be played too quickly. Although there are no fugues in the third and fourth books, Leclair's concern for the avoidance of excessively fast tempos should be carefully noted by present-day performers.

[41]Aldrich feels that appoggiaturas probably never take exactly half the value of the written notes, that they are either a little shorter or a little longer. Personal communication from Putnam Aldrich, Stanford University, Stanford, California, October 19, 1963.

[42]When an appoggiatura is joined to a dotted note, the appoggiatura assumes the value of the main note and the main note receives the value of the dot. See, for example, Leopold Mozart, *A Treatise on the Fundamental Principles of Violin Playing* (1756), trans. Editha Knocker (London: Oxford University Press, 1948), 168.

[43]Quantz, *On Playing the Flute*, 94, footnote 3.

[44]*Ibid.*, 93.

[45]*Ibid.*, 228.

[46]Jean Rousseau, *Traité de la viole* ... (Paris: Christophe Ballard, 1687), 96. Rousseau uses an alternate term, *cheute*, for this ornament.

[47]Jean-Jacques Rousseau, *Dictionnaire de musique*, II, Plate B. The slur in the first part of this example is undoubtedly an error; it should join the small note d″ to the following note.

[48]See, for example, the *Avertissement* in Jacques Boyvin, *Traité abregé de l'accompagnement* ... (Amsterdam: Estienne Roger, c. 1710).

[49]For a corroborating German source, in addition to the Quantz already cited, see Mozart, *A Treatise on the Fundamental Principles of Violin Playing*, 177.

[50]Aldrich, "The Principal *Agréments*," 98.

[51]The omission of a slur does not necessarily mean that a *coulé* is not intended. Slurs are occasionally left out inadvertently, in the first three

books as well as the fourth. To illustrate, slurs are not present in the following example, yet the small notes can surely be performed as true *coulés*.

Opus 9, Sonata 9, *Adagio*, measures 12-13

The problem of interpretation arises when a long slur joins one or more small notes with other, regular notes to form a melodic span, as is illustrated by the examples on page xviii.

⁵²In a recent article Frederick Neumann offers evidence that the French trill may occasionally start on the main note. See "Misconceptions About the French Trill in the 17th and 18th Centuries," *The Musical Quarterly*, L (April, 1964), 188-193.

⁵³Putnam Aldrich, personal communication, October 19, 1963.

⁵⁴Aldrich, "The Principal *Agréments*," 202-203.

⁵⁵*Ibid.*, 238.

⁵⁶Michel Corrette, *L'Ecole d'Orphée méthode pour apprendre facilement à jouer du violon dans le goût françois et italien* . . . (Paris: Chez l'auteur, 1738), 11: "La cadence se prépare toujours par la note Superieure et se marque par un t. ou +."

⁵⁷I do not mean to imply that the trill must be performed precisely as shown in the example; there are several equally correct ways of performing it, but all would commence with a prolongation of the upper appoggiatura—that is, the note with which the trill starts.

⁵⁸Michel Pignolet de Montéclair, *Méthode facile pour aprendre à jouer du violon avec un abrégé des principes de musique necessaires pour cet instrument* (Paris: c. 1712), 9:
Lorsque le tremblement prepare à la cadence, qui est un repose ou chute de chant, il faut le soutenir et le battre egalement et lentement. Soutenir un tremblement c'est poser de d'abord le doit qui doit trembler le rendre immobile pendant la moitié d'un coup d'archet, le trembler sur l'autre moitié, et lever apres avoir tremblé un moment avant que l'archet finisse afin que l'on puisse distinguer la notte sur laquel le tremblement est marqué.

⁵⁹Jean Rousseau, *Traité de la viole*, 83-85.

⁶⁰Aldrich, "The Principal *Agréments*," 246-249.

⁶¹*Ibid.*, 211, 214, 227.

⁶²Aldrich, personal communication, October 19, 1963.

⁶³Montéclair states that the trill before a cadence should be performed "slowly and evenly" (see the full quotation on page xx). A quite different opinion is voiced by Michel de Saint-Lambert in *Les Principes du claveçin* . . . (Paris: Christophe Ballard, 1702), 58:
The number of notes which one must use to execute all ornaments, and the number of times one must play each note, are limited, except in the case of the trill, in which one performs the alteration as quickly as one can; the faster one performs it [the trill] the more notes there will be.
Dans tous les Agrémens, la quantité de Notes qu'on doit emprunter pour les faire & la quantité de fois qu'on les doit toucher sont limitées, excepté seulement dans le Tremblement dont on fait le battement le plus vite qu'on peut; & plus on le fait vîte, plus il y entre de Notes.

In my opinion Saint-Lambert's instructions are inappropriate for the majority of the trills in the Leclair sonatas, especially in slow movements.

⁶⁴Aldrich, "The Principal *Agréments*," 480-482a.

⁶⁵The *clavecin* composers occasionally reduced the speed of the oscillations and occasionally prolonged the oscillation for the whole value of the note—the *pincé continu*. *Ibid.*, 483.

⁶⁶Corrette, *L'Ecole d'Orphée*, 35. Although the example has no key signature, the key of G is apparently assumed; hence the lower auxiliary is f sharp.

⁶⁷Michel Corrette, *L'Art de se perfectionner dans le violon, ou l'on donne a étudier des leçons sur touttes les positions des quatre cordes du violon et les differens coups d'archet* (Paris: Chez l'auteur, c. 1782), 4.

⁶⁸Aldrich, "The Principal *Agréments*," 493-495.

⁶⁹*Ibid.*, 496.

⁷⁰Corrette, *L'Ecole d'Orphée*, 12: "On peut faire des Cadances sur touttes les Notes, mais, l'on en fait jamais trois de suite."

⁷¹See François Couperin, *L'Art de toucher le clavecin* (1717), ed. and trans. into German, Anna Linde; trans. into English, Mevanwy Roberts (Wiesbaden: Breitkopf und Härtel, 1933), 16.

⁷²Aldrich, "The Principal *Agréments*," 536.

⁷³*Ibid.*, 547.

⁷⁴Jean-Jacques Rousseau, *Dictionnaire de musique*, II, Plate B.

⁷⁵Jean Rousseau, *Traité de la viole*, 87: "Le Martellement est toûjours inseparable du Port de Voix, car le Port de voix se doit toûjours terminer par un Martellement."

⁷⁶David Boyden, "The Violin and Its Technique in the 18th Century," *The Musical Quarterly*, XXXVI (January, 1950), 33. Boyden's recent book *The History of Violin Playing from its Origins to 1761 and its Relationship to the Violin and Violin Music* (London: Oxford University Press, 1965) presents a careful study of violin technique in the eighteenth century, including numerous references to Leclair. Persons intending to use this work in connection with the performance of Leclair's sonatas should perhaps be apprised of two errors of fact which it contains. On page 376, Boyden cites Opus 1, Sonata 8, page 77 (of the original edition) as the place where Leclair calls for the use of the thumb; the fingering actually occurs, however, in Sonata 12 of Opus 1, page 77. Boyden's example 189, page 424, is taken from Opus 9, Sonata 4, and Boyden dates the example at *c*. 1730; later, on page 437, he gives the date 1745 for Opus 9. Both dates are incorrect; the opus (the fourth book) was, as I have mentioned above, actually published around 1738.

⁷⁷For an unusual instance of slurred notes bearing strokes see Opus 9, Sonata 8, *Chaconne*, measures 240 and 249.

⁷⁸Sébastien de Brossard, *Dictionaire [sic] de musique*, 3rd ed. (Amsterdam: Roger, n.d.), 134, as quoted in Barbara Seagrave, "The French Style of Violin Bowing and Phrasing from Lully to Jacques Aubert (1650-1730) . . ." (Unpublished dissertation, Stanford University, 1958), 61.

⁷⁹Corrette, *L'Ecole d'Orphée*, 43: "Staccato ou Spiccato, veut dire que les Coups d'Archet . . . doivent être joués secs, sans trainer et bien détachez."

⁸⁰Mozart, *A Treatise on the Fundamental Principles of Violin Playing*, 47. On page 45 Mozart uses slightly different wording, saying that notes with strokes must be "detached from each other by a strong *attack* of the bow in the up stroke. . . ."

⁸¹*Ibid.*, 110. As I have said previously, slurred notes which bear strokes are extremely rare in the Leclair sonatas.

⁸²Quantz, *On Playing the Flute*, 232. Quantz's discussion of the violin, pages 215-237, contains a wealth of interesting information which can be of direct benefit to a violinist performing the Leclair sonatas.

⁸³*Ibid*. Quantz shares Mozart's feeling that notes which bear strokes must be stressed. See, for example, page 224.

⁸⁴Francesco Geminiani, *The Art of Playing on the Violin* (1751), facsimile edited with an introduction by David D. Boyden (London: Oxford University Press, 1952), 8.

⁸⁵*Ibid.*, 27, Example XX.

⁸⁶Jean-Jacques Rousseau, *Dictionnaire de musique*, I, 215: "Genre d'exécution par lequel, au lieu de soutenir des notes durant toute leur valeur, on les sépare par des silences pris sur cette même valeur."

⁸⁷Quantz, *On Playing the Flute*, 232.

⁸⁸*Ibid.*, 221, Figures 17 and 18.

⁸⁹*Ibid*.

⁹⁰Mozart, *A Treatise on the Fundamental Principles of Violin Playing*, 125, Example 8.

⁹¹See, for example, Opus 9, Sonata 5, *Andante*, measures 7, 9, 72, 74 and 75.

⁹²Mozart, *A Treatise on the Fundamental Principles of Violin Playing*, 45. Mozart's treatise contains no dotted notes which are not under slurs.

⁹³Quantz, *On Playing the Flute*, 232.

⁹⁴Corrette, *L'Ecole d'Orphée*, 35: "Nottes égales et articulées d'un même coup d'Archet." In a later violin treatise Corrette states that this type of note should be played "égales, articulées, et un peu détachées." See *L'Art de se perfectionner dans le violon*, 3.

⁹⁵Mozart, *A Treatise on the Fundamental Principles of Violin Playing*, 119.

⁹⁶Boyden, "The Violin and Its Technique," 34. Mondonville's example is reprinted.

⁹⁷Quantz, *On Playing the Flute*, 223.

[98] See, for example, the concluding movements of Sonatas 4, 6, and 7 in the fourth book.

[99] Quantz, *On Playing the Flute*, 217.

[100] The only exceptions are the *tamborins* in which *tasto solo* appears over repeated notes.

[101] Eighteenth-century sources differ as to whether a *tasto solo* may be doubled at the octave. C. P. E. Bach advises against it (see *Essay on the True Art of Playing Keyboard Instruments*, trans. and ed. by William J. Mitchell [New York: W. W. Norton and Co., Inc., 1949], 316); Jean-Jacques Rousseau implies that it is permissible (see the article "*tasto solo*" in *Dictionnaire de musique*, II, 253).

[102] Newman Powell, "Rhythmic Freedom in the Performance of French Music from 1650 to 1735" (Unpublished dissertation, Stanford University, 1958).

[103] Barbara Seagrave, "The French Style of Violin Bowing and Phrasing from Lully to Jacques Aubert (1650-1730): as illustrated in dances from ballets and dance movements from violin sonatas of representative composers" (Unpublished dissertation, Stanford University, 1958).

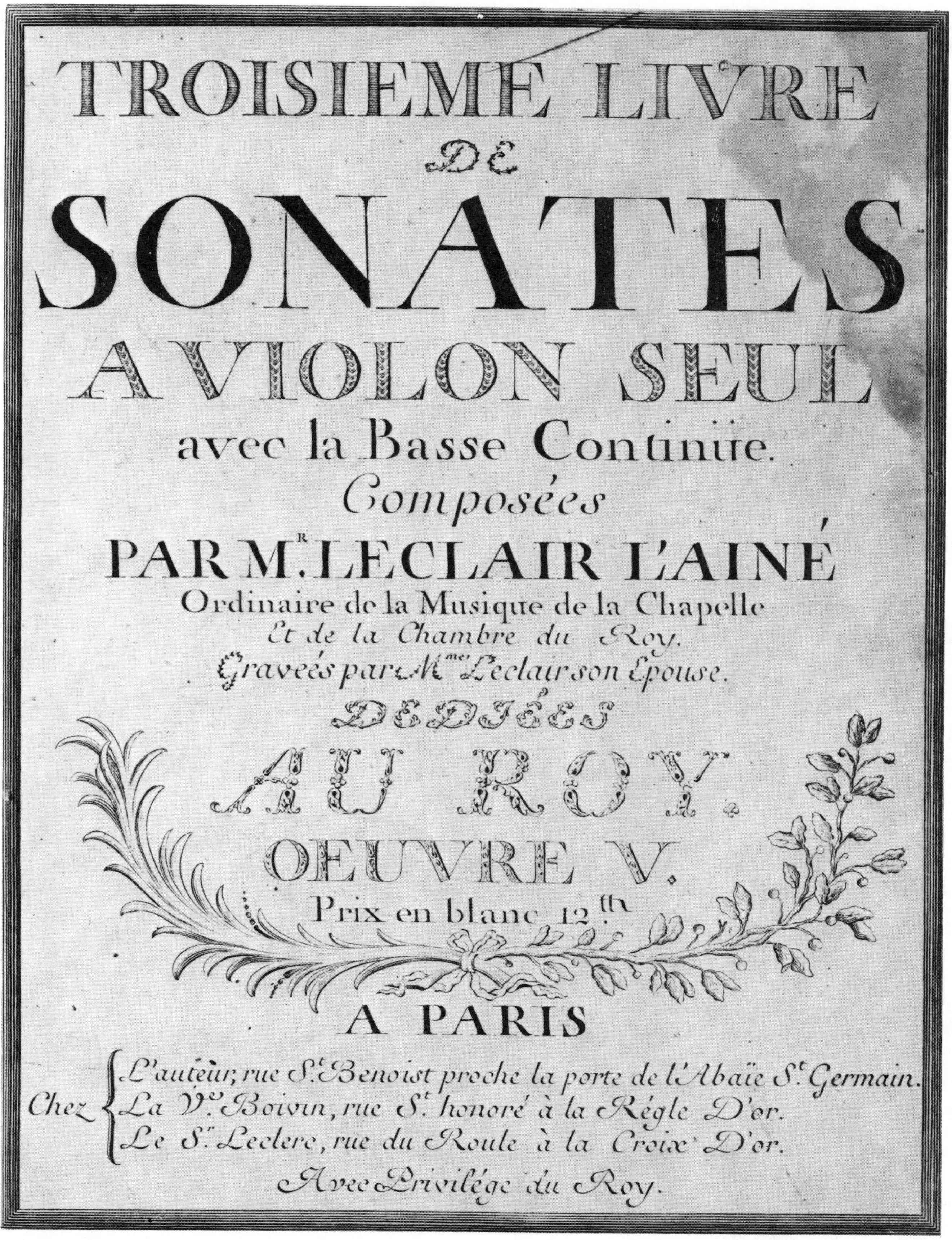

TROISIÈME LIVRE DE SONATES A VIOLON SEUL

avec la Basse Continue.

Composées

PAR M.r LECLAIR L'AINÉ

Ordinaire de la Musique de la Chapelle
Et de la Chambre du Roy.

Gravées par M.me Leclair son Epouse.

DEDIÉES

AU ROY.

OEUVRE V.

Prix en blanc 12.tt

A PARIS

Chez { L'auteur, rue S.t Benoist proche la porte de l'Abaïe S.t Germain.
{ La V.e Boivin, rue S.t honoré à la Régle D'or.
{ Le S.r Leclerc, rue du Roule à la Croix D'or.

Avec Privilége du Roy.

Plate I. *Troisième livre de sonates* . . . , *Oeuvre V:* title page

Plate II. *Troisième livre de sonates . . . , Oeuvre V:* Sonata XII, *Adagio*

SONATAS FOR VIOLIN AND BASSO CONTINUO

Sonata I

(a) The source has *fine* over the first ending, but a new ending is clearly necessary at the conclusion of the movement.

(b) The source gives b', but the consistency of the melodic sequence with that in measures 21 and 22 requires a', which also makes better sense harmonically.

(a) The appoggiatura is c♯″ in the source.

(a) In the source, the figure 3 appears under the quarter-rest, beat 2.

(b) Here and in measures 20, 22, 24, 36, 38, 83, 84, 102, and 104, the source's figures are placed thus: ♪ ♩ ♪ ; it seems likely, however, that the chord changes should occur on the second, third, and fourth eighth-notes.

Sonata II

Sonata III

(a) [dotted eighth-sixteenth rhythm] in the source

(a) The only sixteenth-note appoggiatura in all four books of Leclair's sonatas for violin and continuo; every other appoggiatura is written as an eighth-note.

Sonata IV

(a) ♩ ♫ in the source

48

(a) ♩. ♫ in the source

(a) The separate cello part doubles the keyboard bass for the first twelve measures; it then becomes quite independent, giving the movement the texture of a trio sonata, with two melodic instruments of equal importance supported by a continuo.

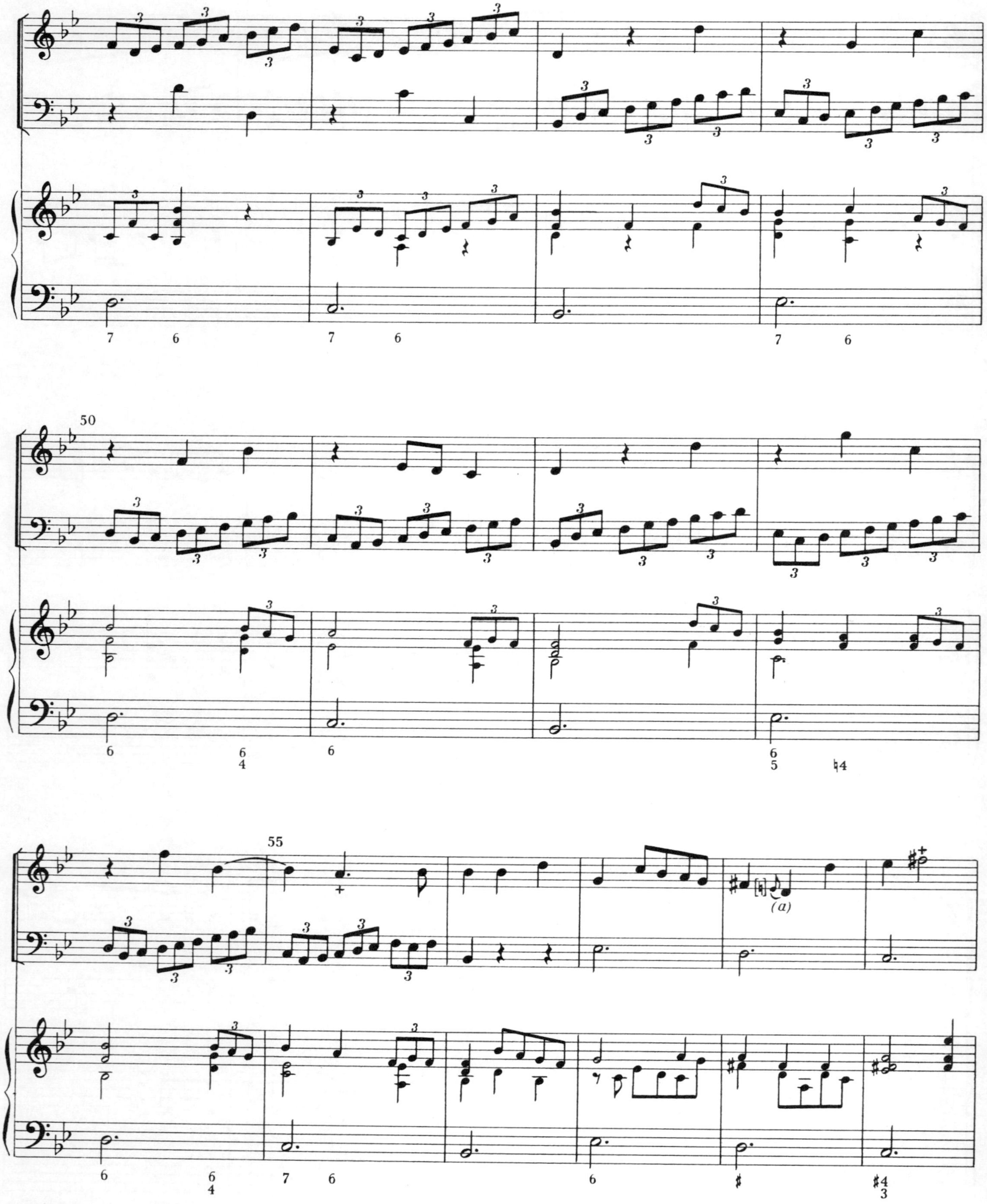

(a) 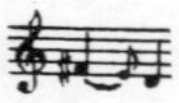 in the source

(a) The words *volti subito,* which accompany a page-turn in the source, imply a warning that the tempo is to remain constant despite the change to the minor mode.

(a) Although the continuo line of this movement has only one note to the measure, chord changes are often called for within a measure, nearly always on the second beat (a chord change on the third beat is specified only in measures 50, 54, and 177). At this point and in measures 99, 101, 102, 103, 137, and 141, however, a chord change on the third beat seems desirable in spite of the placement of the figure in the source.

Sonata V

(a) The four thirty-second notes are cue-sized sixteenths in the source.

(a) Although the violin line consists almost entirely of triplet eighth notes, a duple subdivision of the quarter note seems likely in the upbeats to measures 66 and 96.

(*a*) In the source, some quarter-notes are dotted (*e.g.*, measures 70 and 82) while others are not (*e.g.*, measures 95 and 121). Since Leclair doubtless intends that all quarter notes be of equal duration, dots have been added to those that lack them.